ENDURING
Together

Strength for the
Weary Caregiver

AMY CHASTAIN, RN

Published by hope*books
2217 Matthews Township Pkwy
Suite D302
Matthews, NC 28105
www.hopebooks.com

hope*books is a division of hope*media

Printed in the United States of America

First paperback edition.
Paperback ISBN: 979-8-89185-211-2
Hardcover ISBN: 979-8-89185-153-5
Ebook ISBN: 979-8-89185-154-2
Library of Congress Number: 2025930643

hope*books
hopebooks.com

DISCLAIMER

The content of this book is for informational purposes only and is not intended to diagnose, treat, cure, or prevent any condition or disease. This book is not intended as a substitute for consultation with a licensed practitioner. Please consult with your physician or healthcare specialist regarding any suggestions or recommendations within this book. The author and the publisher assume no responsibility for any injuries suffered or damages incurred during or as a result of the use or application of the information contained herein.

To protect privacy, names and certain details have been altered unless explicit permission has been granted.

In loving memory of my grandmother, Betty (Gigi). Thank you for being my biggest cheerleader, but more importantly, thank you for sharing your heart. Thank you to my family for their endless support and encouragement. I also write for all the caregivers — you are changing the world for the better every single day. I am truly grateful to all the caregivers who shared their stories. Thank you for trusting me.

Praise for Enduring Together

"As a Catastrophic Case Manager, I navigate caregiving's physical, emotional, and spiritual aspects with my patients' families and caregivers. I have also been the caregiver of my younger brother and father, who both died of cancer. I have seen first-hand the emotional highs and lows of caregiving, the lies we tell ourselves, and the physical demands of caring for others and forgetting to care for ourselves. I believe that the best person to write a book for caregiver support is someone who has "walked the walk." Amy has done that through her professional life as an RN and her personal life as a caregiver to her family members.

This book validates and dispels the negative thoughts and lies we tell ourselves as we care for others. Reading this book felt like sitting in my living room, under a warm blanket, talking with my best friend. This book is relatable and is easy to read. But it isn't a book that you read and then forget. It is a book that challenges the reader throughout using simple acronyms that can easily be remembered and reflected upon. It is a book full of "ah ha" moments with moments of validation and support. Amy peels away at the layers of caregiving that hold us back from being true to ourselves while equipping us with tools and new thought processes to be a better caregiver."

Claudine McKemie, M.S., CRC
Catastrophic Case Manager
Certified Rehabilitation Counselor

"If you're wrestling with caregiver fatigue and discouraging days, Amy's *Enduring Together: Strength for the Weary Caregiver* provides a framework to help you discover biblical truths that will encourage your heart and free your mind. Her genuine voice and shared personal experiences will comfort and give care and refreshment to your soul as you serve others."

Hon. Deanna M. Ballard
Former NC State Senator & Samaritan's Purse Executive

"Amy has crafted a beautiful, empathetic resource for caregivers. Through her own experience, she reveals an extraordinary level of insight into the nuances of caregiving. Wrapped in God's truth, readers will find rest for their souls as they traverse the journey of caregiving. I heartily recommend this book to caregivers or those in the caregiving profession."

Dr. Peridot Gilbert-Reed, LPC-S
Registered Play Therapist Supervisor (RPT-S)

"Incredibly refreshing! Author Amy Chastain uses the biblical story of Ruth and Naomi as a guiding narrative to tackle the many lies caregivers often tell themselves and, in turn, believe deep in their souls. These lies can be debilitating if left unchecked. Amy guides the reader to the truth of God's word using real-life examples from her caregiving experiences, encouraging readers to break free of the lies. Do not miss this book!"

Rev. Dr. Aaron C. Moore.
Pastor of Bethel Presbyterian Church in Cornelius, NC.

"As a fellow caregiver, I found this book to be a soothing balm for my weary soul. Chastain skillfully confronts the lies that often plague caregivers, offering instead a path to hope through thoughtful questions, education, and biblical wisdom.

In *Enduring Together*, Amy Chastain pours out her heart, weaving personal experiences with insightful research to create a powerful resource for caregivers. Her writing resonates with authenticity, addressing the multifaceted challenges of caregiving while consistently pointing readers back to the hope found in Scripture.

While each caregiving journey is unique, Chastain's words stirred deep emotions and rang true to my experiences. Her ability to connect with readers, regardless of their circumstances, is remarkable.

Enduring Together is more than just a book; it's a companion for the caregiver's journey. Anyone who has taken on the role of caring for another will find strength, encouragement, and practical guidance within these pages. Chastain's work is a testament to the power of faith, resilience, and the enduring human spirit in the face of life's most challenging responsibilities."

Lisa J Plett
Author of In a *Stroke of Love: Through A Mother's Eyes:*
Hope and Healing on the Special Needs Journey

Table Of Contents

INTRODUCTION

I never dreamt about becoming a nurse, but rather, it came about as my response to a series of hardships that I faced. I witnessed both heartbreak and healing during my time working in the field, and it became clear to me that patients aren't the only ones to suffer. When the Lord called me out of nursing to raise my newly blended family, I struggled to balance my feelings of relief about moving into a more comfortable situation with my feelings of disappointment. It suddenly seemed as though all my hard work and training were going to waste, and I felt that stepping out of the workforce meant I had somehow failed.

Friend, they say that the Lord works in mysterious ways, and I've certainly found this to be true. I "gave up" a nursing career to raise my children but soon found myself thrust into the role of a caregiver. In hindsight, I can see so many ways in which God prepared me for the trials He knew I would face. Although the Lord was always with me, I lost sight of Him as I found myself believing things that were not grounded in His Truth.

I struggled as I battled my thoughts of not being good enough, failure, and comparison. I felt like I was the only one who couldn't get it together and get down to business.

I have walked the hard and holy ground of caregiving and want to help you do the same. Friend, I'm so glad you are here, and I pray that these words can help you find refuge and have respite for your tired and weary soul. Together, we can find our true rest in the Lord. In my many days and nights spent caring for both patients and my own family members, I finally came to realize that while I will always take care of others, the Lord is guiding me to take care of a specific group of people. There is a lot of focus on the people needing physical care, but I believe that God has called me to look further. He wants me to take care of the ones who are at their sides, holding their hands.

I know the exhaustion, despair, loneliness, and overwhelm that comes with caregiving, and I invite you to take my hand and let me help you through it by dispelling the lies we believe with the Truth of God's Word. Whether you are an avid student of the Bible or have never cracked it open, I invite you to lean into the freedom that God's Truth provides.

As caregivers, we come to the rescue of our loved ones, but we are merely shadows of our Savior, Jesus, who redeems all who call on His name. My journey into caregiving began abruptly, and I found myself overwhelmed with new responsibilities. I worked hard to keep up with the changes – to be a good caregiver, wife, mother, daughter, and friend. As a result, I felt like I was disappearing. It seemed as though everything had changed for me, and yet the world around me continued moving on as if nothing had happened. I felt left behind, lost and confused, and in need of rescue.

By returning to the basics of the Truth of God's Word, I was able to gain a foothold from which to climb out of my feelings of hopelessness and despair. Using the REDEEMER framework, throughout the pages of this book, we will learn together to rely on the Word of God by:

1. Recognizing our Value
2. Entrusting Ourselves to the Lord
3. Discerning Needs
4. Engaging in Caregiving

5. Expecting Challenges
6. Meeting People Where They Are, With Mercy
7. Embracing Our Need for Encouragement
8. Remaining Rooted in the Lord

We will address common lies we believe that hinder us from being our best selves and unnecessarily keep us at a distance from our loving Heavenly Father. By learning about His Word and learning to trust in it, we can run out of a place of despair and into a place of hope. And friend, there *is* hope! Join me as we journey out of the dark and scary places and into the light of God. His Truth will dispel the lies we believe in, and by anchoring ourselves to Truth, we can begin to change how we look at things and SHIFT (an acronym) our perspectives.

As a nurse, I worked 12-hour shifts, but as a caregiver, I was always on duty. I know from personal experience that time and energy are in short supply, so I'm including bite-sized actionable information at the end of each chapter to help you get unstuck and move in the right direction. At the end of every chapter, we will address a perspective SHIFT that is available to you in the form of:

SACRIFICE: acknowledging the love offerings that we pour out as we care for others. It is important to recognize them and to account for any losses that we experience.

HOPE: addressing the concept of hope directs our eyes toward the future, which is unknown but secure in God's hands. It helps us figure out where we are struggling and what we need to change and helps us discern what actions we can take to move forward in a positive mindset.

INTERVENTION: an action we take or a mindset shift we engage in to move us out of a place of lonesome struggle and into the peace that only the Lord can give.

FOLLOW-UP: practice your intervention and follow up with an honest assessment of how your situation or heart has changed so that you can keep moving toward the comfort God longs to give you.

TRUST: the basis for strengthening our relationship with the Lord. In this section, we will pour out our hearts in earnest and honest prayer, inviting Him into our hearts and into our hard moments.

Take heart, friend. You are not alone. Together, relying on God, we can break free from the lies that are holding us back. Are you ready to jump in?

PART 1

RECOGNIZE YOUR VALUE

"For he chose us in him before the creation of the world to be holy and blameless in his sight. In love he predestined us for adoption to sonship through Jesus Christ, in accordance with his pleasure and will."
— Ephesians 1:4-5

CHAPTER 1

VALUE BEYOND EARNING

"There are four kinds of people in the world – those who have been caregivers, those who are currently caregivers, those who will be caregivers, and those who will need caregivers."
–Rosalynn Carter[1]

I gave myself a pep talk as I walked the halls of the hospital in the middle of the night. It was more than that, really; my internal dialogue had morphed from a pep talk into a lecture about bucking up. "What is wrong with you?" I asked myself. "Pull yourself together!" I proclaimed. "This building is full of people dealing with worse things than you, and they are soldiering on, not drowning in despair," I ridiculed. But there I was — drowning underwater.

I quietly paced the floors, passing nurses at their stations and maintenance workers cleaning the tile. I passed rooms full of patients, but still, the solitude was overwhelming. Visiting hours were over. I was alone physically, as well as alone with my thoughts — these ugly, unhelpful feelings that wouldn't subside. And in the quiet of the night, when everything else hushed, my emotions became loud and intrusive.

Daybreak came, and the parade of doctors and nurses and patient care techs commenced. It wouldn't be long before my family and friends started texting or calling me. "How are you?" they would ask. That's a hard question to answer before I've even finished the hospital-grade cup of coffee. Most of the time, my answer was something to the effect of, "I'm hanging in there." It wasn't really a lie; I'd just call it more of a programmed response. At least, that's what I told myself. As my grandfather would have said, I was on the right side of the grass. He loved to use this saying when someone was complaining, making the point that things could always be worse – "At least you aren't dead!" I didn't feel fantastic, but I'd had a shower and some food and had managed to catch a few hours of sleep.

Occasionally, I would imagine answering the question with brutal honesty. How am I feeling? "I'm frustrated, anxious, angry, fearful, impatient, despondent, exhausted, overwhelmed, helpless, hopeless — need I go on?" But nobody wants to hear that, or so I thought. Those feelings were so big and untamed that it felt wrong for me to let them even cross my mind. Surely, I shouldn't let others in on the secret that deep down, I felt like a horrible person, like a weakling — one who isn't nearly as strong as she needs to be.

In times of doubt or struggle, I find myself returning to familiar and encouraging Scripture passages. I'm especially drawn to stories of hope in the midst of heartbreak, and the book of Ruth is one of my favorites. Throughout these pages, we will explore the book of Ruth, learn about the power of love and faithfulness, and see that even God's chosen women lacked understanding from time to time. If you are unfamiliar with this Bible story, I invite you to read it – it's not very long, but it is rich in wisdom.

Ruth's story explores grief, doubt, God's provision, and also speaks to complex issues about identity. What does it mean to be a wife or a widow or a foreigner? What does it mean when everything familiar is suddenly stripped away by changing circumstances? How can we grow in the knowledge that our identity is in Christ and is not determined by our relationship to those around us?

Let me ask you another question: have you ever felt invisible? I don't mean in a good way, like when you were a kid and had the childish delights of an imaginary cloak of invisibility. That would be magical and empowering, and who among us hasn't wished for superpowers at some point in our lives? No, what I'm referring to is the feeling you get when you know people can physically see you, but at the same time, they're looking right past you. This sensation is distinct from feeling transparent. When someone sees through you, they take note of your presence and your heart. Someone looking past you is different; it's a lonely feeling, confirming our fears that we aren't worth being noticed, as if we are undeserving of truly being seen. I felt smaller by the day as I stepped fully into my role as a caregiver. The long-held fear of not being enough transformed from a whisper to a shout, all while I worked tirelessly to put the needs of others above my own, and I felt like I was disappearing into the backdrop of life.

I remember asking myself many times, *How did I end up here?* I'll admit that these feelings of insignificance were self-produced. Nobody was putting me down or treating me as if I were inferior in any way. No, this was a dark shadow of a longing in my heart: to be known and loved and accepted – just as I am. Instead, I felt worthless, invisible, insignificant. I didn't even feel like myself anymore. My entire existence seemed to revolve around taking care of other people, and I started to feel like I had no real purpose, and perhaps even scarier, I wasn't doing anything to prove my worth. The lie that I wasn't valuable had taken hold of my heart.

Throughout my 15 years as a caregiver, I was confronted with this lie and many others like it. I have never felt so alone, so isolated, and so afraid. There were many days when I felt not only helpless but hopeless. But as challenging as this season was, I wouldn't trade it for anything because it was through this time that God lit a fire in my heart to be a voice of hope and truth for other caregivers. He called me to help dismantle the lies the enemy injects with the Truth of who God says you are based on His Word. With that said, I'd like to share with you the first lie the enemy used to break down my sense of value and worth.

LIE #1: I AM NOT VALUABLE

Are you an overachiever by any chance? Well, I'll go ahead and raise my hand high in answer to that question, as it very much describes me. I don't like being the center of attention, but I do enjoy feeling competent. It's been this way for as long as I can remember. I was the kid in high school known as the "smart, quiet one," which might sound nice as an adult, but as a teenager, I wanted to be the "fun, popular girl." Alas, it was not to be. To this day, I'm the boring, hard-working, get-it-done team player. And I'm fine with it now, but I've come to realize something important: I don't feel valuable when I don't have things that document my accomplishments. I seem to require some sort of outside "proof" to believe I have worth. Somewhere along the way, I bought into the lie that achievement equals value.

This measuring system seemed to serve me well as a student. I could believe that I had worth because my grade point average said so. I was able to maintain this facade throughout my life as I continued hitting all the traditional milestones, moving from young adulthood into being a full-blown grown-up: graduating college, finding a job, getting married, and having children. Check! I was doing all the things that the outside world expected of me. But I had a secret — deep down, I didn't believe that I was good enough. And somehow, I reasoned, if I'm not good enough, then maybe I'm not worth anything at all.

I harbored that secret for a long time before I truly stumbled over it. As the years passed, my role in the family changed. I became a stay-at-home mother and loved it (most of the time, anyway). Who needs a report card when you are doing what you love, right? Well, I came to find out I still did. Without realizing it, I was still buying into the lie that I had to prove myself to those around me to have value, and it was exhausting. Do you ever feel that if you work a little harder, do things a little better, or get more organized, people will recognize your worth? It's exhausting, isn't it?

I soon discovered that caring for children and caring for adults are different animals. Whereas I felt relatively confident in my role as a mother, I felt timid and unsure when I stepped up to care for adults. I came to nursing as a second career when I was in my 30s, and I remember feeling intimidated when I was learning to go into patient rooms and conduct hands-on assessments. As with most things, practice and repetition helped me feel more confident in my abilities. It wasn't long before I stepped away from the nursing profession and found myself back in a home setting where my job as a mom quickly morphed into caregiver of adults. Tasks that were routine as an RN seemed awkward as a family caregiver. In some ways, people expected more from me because of my professional background. However, the dynamics and nuances of caring for a stranger in a hospital setting are quite different from those involved when caring for a loved one in their own home. I was supposed to be the perfect caregiver, which was, of course, an unattainable goal; I had just set myself up for more failure. As I struggled to meet everyone's needs while often ignoring my own, I became fatigued, disconnected, and tiptoed right up to the line of hopelessness. I desperately wanted to demonstrate my worthiness, but I felt like I just couldn't keep going. Finally, I crashed. It seemed to me that I was failing at everything, and I had convinced myself that I was a disappointment to everyone, including God.

As I sat with the weight of these feelings, it felt like they were going to crush me. Finally, with my defenses totally worn down,

I lay on the floor of my living room, surrendering first to the tears and finally to the Lord. As I sobbed, I felt a nudge from the Holy Spirit asking, "What does God say about you?"

It is a wonderful question. What *does* God say about me, I wondered? As I dove into Scripture, I found the life-altering answer my soul desperately needed at that moment. It's this verse that has since carried me forward, countering the lie that my life isn't valuable. Here is what God says about me and about you, my friend. He says you are created in His image; you are a daughter of the King. You are chosen. Psalm 139:13-15 explains this beautifully,

> *"For you created my inmost being; you knit me together in my mother's womb. I praise you because I am fearfully and wonderfully made; your works are wonderful, I know that full well. My frame was not hidden from you when I was made in the secret place, when I was woven together in the depths of the earth."*

The Bible is full of passages that communicate God's great love for us. Am I the only one who has struggled to accept this enormous gift without feeling like there must be some sort of quid-pro-quo?

Over time, I was able to see that I was in dire need of a change in my perspective. I began to realize I shouldn't be asking: *What is wrong with me?* But rather, *what is wrong with my situation?* I realized I had been looking at things from a very narrow perspective, and this newfound awareness began a shift in me that changed everything.

Imagine standing on a sidewalk in a busy city and looking up at the skyscraper next to you. The building will likely seem imposing, and you may even experience a sense of vertigo as you crane your head to see the top of the structure. Now, imagine standing on the roof of that skyscraper and looking out over the horizon. Your view is very different. Perspective matters. I realized that I had been filtering everything through my self-centered, individual perspective rather than trying to see things through God's eyes. I finally began to understand that I was not designed to shoulder the weight of the world by myself. This situation of becoming a full-time caregiver and carrying the weight on my own was above my pay grade. And the good news, my friend, is that it's above yours too. There is hope for you even in the midst of this challenging, unexpected season you find yourself in. God values you as His beloved daughter and longs to care for you as you care for them... you need only let Him.

I wish I could tell you that in a singular moment, my heart was completely transformed, but it wasn't. It takes time. I did, however, realize my need to begin with the Truth of the Lord. I needed to seek the Scriptures expressing His feelings for me, and I needed to be honest with Him that I was having trouble imprinting that Truth on my heart. Try as I might, I continued to fight with a stubborn nugget of doubt that insisted I had to respond to His love by proving I was worth it.

Friend, are you struggling with this same thing in your caregiving journey? Please, have hope. A lifetime of faith is referred to as a "walk with Jesus" for a reason. It is a compilation of learning and growth that takes place over time as we dwell in our relationship with Him. He knows our struggles, our doubts, and our deep, dark fears, and still, He loves us. The truth is that we don't have to earn His love.

There are many things in life that we do need to earn, and it starts when we are very young. A preschool teacher might award the position of line leader to the child who sat still and listened attentively during story time. The fifth-grade student with good social and athletic skills will likely be selected as team captain for the recess games. Orchestra students must perform to get their seats assigned, and nobody earns the first chair by skipping out on practice all the time. Oh, and the grades — such a source of stress and anxiety for these students with their eyes on the future! College applications, standardized test scores, and extracurricular activities all feel monumentally weighty at that age. Our pattern of earning things does not disappear as we enter adulthood. Are we trustworthy? Dependable? Hard-working? Do we have what it takes to climb the corporate ladder? Our boss probably wants proof of our abilities.

Yes, we have a great deal of practice in earning things. It's what we are used to, and it's how we view the world. Please hear this good news: we do not have to earn the love of God. This is especially awesome because we wouldn't be capable of earning it even if we wanted to.

> *"For God so loved the world, that he gave his only Son, that whoever believes in him should not perish but have eternal life."*
>
> –John 3:16

Jesus made a way for us. There is no need to earn God's love because it is a gift freely given. Does that mean we should take it for granted, push it away, or dismiss it? Absolutely not. It does mean that His love is unconditional. Would you stop loving your child if he did something stupid? No. Would you want him to learn to do what is good for him and those around him? Yes. God desires for us to draw near to Him and to love Him with all our hearts.

> *"Draw near to God and he will draw near to you."*
>
> –James 4:8, ESV

My friend, your role as a caregiver does not mean you are worthless, nor does it mean you are worth *less*. Our value comes from the Lord Almighty–not from our coworkers or our neighbors or our loved ones. We do not have to prove our worthiness to God, as He knows our true value. When those moments of self-doubt come prowling, remember to start with the Truth. Jesus paid the price for us — for our sins, failures, and bad attitudes — and we are the precious children of the Lord Most High, even on our worst days. He wants us to walk with Him, abide in Him, and be in a close relationship with Him. And He loves us even when we fail to do so. You are valued more deeply than you can even know, and *that* is the truth.

PERSPECTIVE SHIFT:

The demands and challenges we face as caregivers are ongoing, but we can reframe our experience by shifting our perspective. By learning to view our situation through the lens of God's Word and by leaning into the Truth it provides, we can begin to move from feeling fearful to hopeful, from embattled to empowered in Christ, and from unseen to unconditionally loved.

SACRIFICE: Sacrifices are the love offerings that we pour out as we care for others, and it is important to recognize them and to account for any losses that we experience.

Write down one or two things that made you feel valuable that you have given up fulfilling caregiving duties. How do you feel about these sacrifices?

HOPE: Addressing the concept of hope directs our eyes toward the future, which is unknown but secure in God's hands. It helps us figure out where we are struggling, what we need to change, and helps us discern what actions we can take to move forward in a positive mindset.

What does God want you to know about how He sees you?

Check out the following verses:

Zephaniah 3:17

Jeremiah 31:3

1 John 3:1

INTERVENTION: Intervention is an act we take or a mindset shift we engage in to move us out of a place of lonesome struggle and into the peace that only the Lord can give.

Counter your false thoughts with scriptural truth. Pick a verse to memorize (or write it down and keep it close at hand) for moments when you struggle to understand that you are a precious daughter of the King.

FOLLOW-UP: Practice your intervention and follow up with an honest assessment of how your situation or heart has changed so that you can keep moving toward the comfort God longs to give you.

How has speaking and reading the Word of God changed your thought process?

TRUST: Trust is the basis for strengthening our relationship with the Lord. In this section, we will pour out our hearts in earnest and honest prayer, inviting Him into our hearts and into our hard moments.

Heavenly Father, help us to truly know how very much You love us. We trust Your Word even when the lies of the enemy seep into our minds. Cover us, we pray, with Your love and protection. Guard our hearts, Lord, that we may always remember to look to You for the Truth.

Amen.

CHAPTER 2

CAREGIVERS ARE KINGDOM WORKERS

---

*"Nowadays people know the price of everything
and the value of nothing."*
—Oscar Wilde[1]

I walked confidently into the swanky downtown restaurant, happy that I had nailed the unspoken dress code with my gray sheath dress and pearls. My husband and I had been invited to a bipartisan political gathering, and upon arrival, we were met with a room full of well-dressed people and fancy food. "This should be fun," I thought to myself. Sister, was I ever wrong.

"What do you do?" the gentleman next to me asked. I pulled out my speech about taking care of kids and family, and I could practically see his eyes glaze over. He gave a polite response and quickly moved on to find another conversational partner. The evening continued on with similar interactions. To add icing on the cake, the person who invited us introduced us this way: "This is my friend John, the tech genius. Oh, and this is his wife, Amy." Womp, womp, womp. I could feel my confidence leaving me like helium from a deflating balloon.

I am shy by nature, and I felt increasingly out of place as the evening wore on. I met local and state officials, attorneys, CEOs, and entrepreneurs, and I struggled with the feeling that I just didn't belong. It is natural for people to talk about their jobs, but the evening taught me that while I certainly wasn't ashamed of being a caregiver, I wasn't exactly proud of it, either.

Modern society holds certain occupations in high esteem: professional athletes, famous actors and musicians, CEOs, and other high-powered, high-earning executives. We live in a culture that places special recognition on individuals who produce. We like to "ooh" and "ahh" over the latest sell-out tour, the game with record-breaking attendance, or the newest gadget from the tech titans. It's an ongoing battle to outdo ourselves and each other, but the reality is that most of us won't ever travel in the circles of the rich and famous. Caregivers are not only *not* famous but often anonymous and unappreciated.

So, let's start with learning who caregivers are. We are the face of our community. We come from all racial and ethnic groups, all socioeconomic statuses, and every religion. We are women and men, young and not so young. We are working, and we are retired. We are single, married, divorced, and widowed. We often take care of parents, spouses, siblings, or other loved ones, sometimes while still raising our own children. Some of us are in this for the long haul, while others will serve for a shorter season.

Here are some quick facts about caregivers:[2]

- A caregiver is defined as an adult who has provided unpaid care to an adult or a child with a medical, behavioral, or other condition or disability at some point during the last 12 months.
- 1 in 5 Americans are a caregiver (53 million people).

As a group, caregivers are growing, and demographic trends indicate that we will continue to add numbers to our ranks. What's driving the increase in the number of caregivers? Simply put, our population is aging. Baby boomers (those born between 1946 and 1964) began turning 65 in the year 2011. This generation drove increased demand in everything from education to housing as they grew up, and now, they will drive demand for healthcare services.[3]

Most people will be touched by caregiving at some point in their lives, and for this reason, I believe we need to get better at addressing the hardships that caregivers face. Caregiving tends to be undervalued by society at large. Our work is unpaid and thereby seen as insignificant. The reality is that caregiving is valuable both in an economic and moral sense. Caregivers are kingdom workers. Regardless of how society views us, we now know that our value is God-given and not earned. We know God loves and values us, but sometimes, we buy into the next deceptive belief.

LIE #2: CAREGIVING IS NOT VALUABLE

The world doesn't stop spinning when we step into our roles as caregivers. Bosses still expect us to show up to work, schools continue to require students to come to class on time, and dinner doesn't magically cook itself. We find ourselves in unfamiliar territory, and it feels simultaneously like everything has changed and nothing has changed. We can struggle to adjust to additional demands on our time while trying to prioritize the needs of those around us. We give of ourselves until it hurts, and because caregiving is unprofitable, we can begin to believe it lacks value.

Pamela's Story:

Pamela was working in a demanding position at a mortgage company when her mother became unable to care for herself. Luckily, Pamela was able to share caregiving duties with her sister. They juggled schedules and their young children and did their best to make the household run smoothly, even hiring an outside caregiver to check on Mom while they were at work. Pamela couldn't keep up with the pace of needs both professionally and in her personal life, and she made the decision to change her job responsibilities so that she could provide the care that her mom needed. This change at work came with a pay cut, leading to finances being extra tight just when expenses were piling up. Pamela made these changes willingly, stating that her mother had to come first, but she recognized that she sacrificed some of her financial security and professional opportunities to do so.

Pamela's story is not unusual. Time is a limited resource, and unlike love, we can't just manufacture more of it. Time is more like a pie that we must slice up, and if someone gets a giant piece, the other pieces are bound to be smaller. This, of course, leads to difficult decisions for many of us. How are we supposed to choose between taking care of Dad or making sure we can still afford for our child to play fall soccer?

Family caregivers are the glue holding millions of families together, sometimes at great personal cost. Yet, we are often overlooked when it comes to healthcare expenses.

Discussions revolve around hospital care, rehabilitation facilities, nursing homes, memory care, home health, and assisted living. These are all important pieces of healthcare infrastructure; rightly, there is a public focus on such systems' economic realities and sustainability. However, the truth of the matter is that for all the good things about our healthcare system, it is also very fractured. We have a shortage of resources for the needs we are currently experiencing, and though the workforce of direct care workers is projected to grow, we also need to acknowledge the high turnover rate for these jobs, which ranges from 40-60%.[4] Even now, we are not keeping up. Perhaps, like me, you have also seen firsthand the worrying staffing shortages in memory care facilities or watched friends struggle as they tried to find rehab placement for their parents.

Direct care workforce shortages are widespread. Many factors go into the workplace shortage, but low pay, difficult work environments, and high turnover are major contributors. Let's imagine that a memory care facility hires a new Certified Nursing Assistant (CNA). She starts her new job in an understaffed nursing home, which can lead to insufficient training and onboarding. She is now asked to care for more patients than guidelines recommend. She faces a situation where mistakes are more likely, injuries (to herself or the patient) are more likely, and poor performance overall is more likely. It is rare for a person to be thrown into such a suboptimal position and be able to thrive in her job duties. She is caught in a negative feedback loop. The unpleasant and sometimes unsafe work environment leads her to resign. This results in even fewer staff for the same amount of work, which increases the difficulty of an already challenging job. A diminished work environment makes it harder to hire new qualified staff successfully.

Family caregivers provide an average of 18 hours of care per week, which translates to an estimated 36 billion hours of unpaid care per year.[5] Caring for someone 18 hours a week may sound manageable, or it may sound overwhelming. It could be both or either during any given week. My mother-in-law, Jackie, was fortunate enough to find a caregiver to assist her when my father-in-law struggled with Alzheimer's. Anxiety caused him to seek the comfort of her presence – constantly. If she went to the bedroom, he went to the bedroom. When she wanted to go for a walk, he wanted to join her. If she was behind a closed bathroom door, he was right there waiting for her when she opened it. Jackie was feeling frazzled one afternoon and decided that what she really needed was a few minutes to herself while the caregiver looked after my father-in-law. She stealthily went into the kitchen, made herself a peanut butter and jelly sandwich, and grabbed a Diet Coke® from the refrigerator before sneaking down to a basement storage room. She deadpanned as she recounted the events of the day: "And he FOUND me down there!"

It's normal to need a break – even from your husband, your child, or your best friend. Many caregivers struggle with feelings of guilt when they decide they need to hire help. Friend, please hear me: caregiving is valuable in and of itself. Hiring additional caregivers does not take away from what you are providing for your loved one.

Many of us need to supplement our own efforts with paid help, which can be hard to find. Did you know that when families are unable to secure paid help for caregiving needs, a member of the family ends up doing *more* unpaid work? That's right – even if you have the money to spend on a professional caregiver, you may not be able to hire one. If you need to move your loved one into a full-time care facility, space may not be available. Guess who will end up shouldering that extra load? Yes, I'm looking at you, my friend.

Caregivers are a quiet economic powerhouse and provided an estimated $600 billion worth of care in 2021.[6] That's right, a billion with a "B." I don't know about you, but that sure sounds valuable to me. And as mind-boggling as that number is, it does not capture the entirety of the value that caregivers are providing. Caregivers sacrifice not only their time and talent but their treasure as well. Dollar estimates do not account for the opportunity costs paid by caregivers. Most caregivers are employed, and over half of them work in hourly wage positions.[7] People who work for an hourly wage often have less flexibility to adapt their working hours to the needs of their families. That said, even a great work situation can become tenuous if the caregiver is frequently late, absent, distracted, or otherwise viewed as unreliable. One in ten working caregivers remove themselves from the workforce by resigning or retiring early.[8] This has financial consequences for caregivers and their families. In addition, time spent away from work due to caregiving responsibilities can result in missed promotions or other opportunities for career advancement.

Some caregivers step out of the workforce for a season, but this, too, has consequences. Much like women who remove themselves from the workforce to raise children, caregivers can run up against difficulty finding employment when they are able to revisit the job market. Not only have they missed out on wages they would have made if they were working instead of caregiving, but they have also missed months or even years of experience, which will affect their earning potential from here on out. Caregiving for a season can have long-term financial impacts. Even eventual social security benefits can be affected by absence from the workplace during the adult years.

Despite economic challenges, by and large, we keep walking the road of caregiving. The journey is neither easy nor predictable, but it is important. The value of caregiving is so much more than dollars and cents. How do you put a price tag on Dad continuing to live in his own home, or the comfort you bring when you hold your daughter's hand while she receives her chemotherapy infusion or the life-giving encouragement you give your husband while he battles kidney failure? Caregivers are redeemers; we are called to bring help, healing, and hope. Jesus is our ultimate Redeemer, but He can use us to shine His light and reflect His love. God sees you, and He sees your work. Let's look at the following Scripture passage to see what the Lord teaches us about the value of caregiving:

> *"The King will reply, 'Truly I tell you, whatever you did for one of the least of these brothers and sisters of mine, you did for me.'"*
>
> –Matthew 25:40

Would you clean a wound for Jesus? Would you feed Him if He couldn't eat? Can you imagine what an honor it would be to physically minister to your Savior? This is how Jesus views caregiving – as if we were doing it for Him personally.

Unpaid caregivers make enormous contributions to our society, both economically and emotionally. We are valuable in a secular sense, but more importantly, we are valuable because God says we are. 1 Peter 2:9 tells us,

> *"But you are a chosen people, a royal priesthood, a holy nation, God's special possession, that you may declare the praises of him who called you out of darkness into his wonderful light."*

You (yes, you, who often feel unseen and unknown) are God's special possession, part of His chosen people. Just as importantly, the people you take care of are also children of the King, and He sees how they are treated. As God's chosen people, we can find peace in His abounding and abiding love. We find value in caregiving when we view it through the lens of God's Word. The work you are doing is hard and holy, scary and sacred, and it has eternal impact. Be encouraged today; caregiving holds a value that can't be fully measured here on earth. The value is eternal and is seen through the eyes of our loving Father.

PERSPECTIVE SHIFT:

The demands and challenges we face as caregivers are ongoing, but we can reframe our experience by shifting our perspective. By learning to view our situation through the lens of God's Word and by leaning into the Truth it provides, we can begin to move from feeling fearful to hopeful, from embattled to empowered in Christ, and from unseen to unconditionally loved.

SACRIFICE: What are some of the economic challenges you have faced as a caregiver?

HOPE: What do you hope those sacrifices will achieve?

INTERVENTION: Educate yourself about the economic challenges of caregiving and learn to speak truth when presented with situations or people that dismiss/demean the value of caregiving.

FOLLOW-UP: Evaluate your feelings about the value of caregiving. How have they changed?

TRUST: *Lord, help us to remember that You will direct our steps. You will make our paths straight. We trust that You see and value both our hearts and the work of our hands.*

Amen.

PART 2

ENTRUST YOURSELF TO THE LORD

"But blessed is the one who trusts in the Lord, whose confidence is in him. They will be like a tree planted by the water that sends out its roots by the stream. It does not fear when heat comes; its leaves are always green. It has no worries in a year of drought and never fails to bear fruit."

— Jeramiah 17:7-8

CHAPTER 3

THE COMPARISON TRAP

"Comparison is the thief of joy."
–Theodore Roosevelt[1]

*H*as caregiving left you tired? I don't mean sleepy. Are you experiencing weariness that is so deep you can feel it in your bones? Does it feel like the troubles you carry are pushing you deeper and deeper into the dirt? I had so many days when I felt that way in my caregiving journey. It seemed like no matter how hard I worked, I still couldn't get everything done. And to make matters worse, I would look around and notice that other people seemed to be managing just fine. It made me wonder, *"What is wrong with me?"*

I was in a vulnerable place. Caregiving had taken away my routine and my sense of stability. Instead of seeking the Lord, I turned inward for a solution. I was going to plow through this season of challenge with willpower. Other people do this every day, I reasoned. It made sense to try and figure out how they were functioning successfully. I fell into the comparison trap.

LIE #3: SOMEONE ELSE CAN DO IT BETTER

"Anything girls can do, boys can do better!" hollered the rowdy group of boys. The girls quickly answered back, "Girls go to college to get more knowledge, boys go to Jupiter to get more stupider!" Comparison and one-upmanship are universal, and they start on the playground.

Sometimes, comparison is helpful. A young child will observe a parent doing housework and seek to replicate the action. Comparison can lead to imitation, or at least our best attempts at it. More often, however, comparison is a trap that can lead to envy, judgment, or pride. As caregivers, it's easy to fall into the trap of believing someone else can do it better. We measure our current struggles against our perceptions of how other caregivers handle their roles. They may appear as "super-caregivers," and we seem to pale in comparison.

The Bible demonstrates the dangers of comparison in the book of Genesis. Joseph was the youngest brother of the family and the favorite son of his father, Jacob. His older brothers were aware of Joseph's favored status. Let's take a look at what Scripture says:

> "Now Israel loved Joseph more than any of his other sons, because he had been born to him in his old age; and he made an ornate robe for him. When his brothers saw that their father loved him more than any of them, they hated him and could not speak a kind word to him."
>
> – Genesis 37:3-4

We often compare ourselves to others because we aren't perfect, and we are not fully entrusting ourselves to the Lord. Joseph's brothers were competing for their father's love, and it led to horrible acts of violence against Joseph. Is it possible that we compare ourselves to others because we are competing for *our* Heavenly Father's love? And, if so, what might that be doing to our own hearts? Proverbs 4:23 tells us, "Above all else, guard your heart, for everything you do flows from it."

As a child, I'll never forget the arguments I would get into with my brother. "That's not fair!" my brother and I would exclaim as we worked on the task. The challenge? We needed to divide a singular piece of Hubba Bubba® gum evenly. My mother (either very wise or an evil genius) had decreed that one piece was too big for one child. We had to share it, and we had to figure that out on our own, or else... no gum for us. In the beginning, my mother would cut the gum in half, and we would proceed to compare the resulting pieces, each of us claiming that the other had the larger piece of gum. Finally, Mom grew tired of this and washed her hands of the aggravation. Her suggestion: one of you cut it, and the other one gets to choose first.

We often associate complaints of unfairness with immaturity, but the truth is that human beings are prone to comparing themselves to others, no matter our ages. We compare ourselves to others: what we have, what we do, where we live, where we go, and what we drive. The struggle is real, and comparison is a dangerous thing to play with. We use a worldly measuring stick, and we often feel that we come up lacking. Comparison can drive a wedge between otherwise loving family members or friends. It creates a hostile environment of one-upmanship. We measure, and we judge, even about petty things.

As caregivers, we might compare our efforts with those of a sibling and make statements like, "I took Mom to three medical appointments last month, and you only took her to one," or, "I was up twice during the night taking care of Dad while you got a good night of sleep."

Comparison turns our hearts ever inward and leaves less and less room for grace as it grows. I've even heard caregivers argue over who did a better job at preventing pressure ulcers from plaguing their loved ones! Caregiving is stressful at the best of times, and arguing about who is better at preventing bedsores is counterproductive. The reality is that in most circumstances, comparing ourselves to other people will not help us achieve our desired outcomes. Assessment is important, but there is a difference between learning about and implementing best practices versus fussing with other caregivers about who is best at each task. Often, the underlying insult is the insinuation that the caregiver who performs the best or does the most loves the care recipient more than the other person does. To our ears, competition or criticism can sometimes sound like, "I love her more than you do!" Yikes!

It's so easy to fall into the misconception that God rewards those He loves and punishes those who anger Him or to believe that He will love us more if we do all the right things. The love and the discipline of the Lord are not so easily explained. How often have you sat in a hospital room, a waiting room, or at a bedside and silently cried out to the Lord: *What did I do to deserve this? Why are you doing this to my loved one?*

I've had more of those moments than I care to admit. In the dark moments, I even wondered: how could a loving God do this to His children? It didn't make sense to me. I was struggling to trust in Him when I didn't understand His ways. My friend, we are not alone in these feelings. The book of Ruth gives us a view into the lives of many people – flawed, emotional, real people.

The saga begins with a family who flees famine in Bethlehem and travels to Moab. They settle in the foreign land, but over the years, tragedy strikes, and the matriarch, Naomi, is left alone and unprotected. Having experienced a great deal of misfortune over the years, Naomi concludes that the Lord had turned against her. God blessed Naomi by having Ruth accompany her back to Bethlehem, but Naomi was focused only on the things that had been removed from her.

> "So the two women went on until they came to Bethlehem. When they arrived in Bethlehem, the whole

town was stirred because of them, and the women exclaimed, 'Can this be Naomi?' 'Don't call me Naomi,' she told them. 'Call me Mara, because the Almighty has made my life very bitter. I went away full, but the Lord has brought me back empty. Why call me Naomi? The Lord has afflicted me; the Almighty has brought misfortune upon me.'"

– Ruth 1:19-21

Maybe you can identify with Naomi in this story. We know that God loves us and that we should trust Him. Naomi knew it, too, but she stumbled when confronted with ongoing grief and hardship. I imagine that Naomi looked around at her peers, the women who still had their husbands and children, and felt slighted. She lamented that God had turned against her, implying recognition that her situation differed from those of the other women. If her grief or hardship had been collective, she probably wouldn't have felt singled out, but she fell into the comparison trap. Is this a familiar struggle for you as well? Naomi viewed her difficulties as misfortunes that God brought upon her, not as regular adversities of earthly life. She failed to recognize that God never left her and that she was the one who took her eyes off Him.

If we aren't careful to keep our eyes on God, we can fall prey to the trap of comparison. It's especially easy to slip into that behavior when life seems unfair. It's easy for us to look around and wonder why other people have it so easy, but it can also work in the other direction. I found myself confronted with this truth one day as I navigated my son's hospitalization. I was frustrated, tired, and frankly, feeling rather sorry for myself. My son was debilitated with vomiting and severe headaches. We had been in the hospital for nearly a week, and the doctors still didn't have a good explanation for what was wrong. I became angry with God as I watched my son suffer through his pain. It wasn't fair.

I decided that it would be good for my son to get out of his hospital room and see something besides the same four walls. I coaxed him into getting up, loaded him in a wheelchair, and traveled down to the children's area so he could meet the therapy dogs. I was understandably feeling stressed after multiple days in the hospital, but as I wheeled my son into the room, I took a hard look around. There was a young boy there with screws and rods coming out of his bones. Another child appeared to have some sort of serious head injury. It was like a slap in the face to me. "Wow," I thought to myself, "I should not be stressed about my son. Those poor kids have *real* problems!" Have you fallen for this one? The "other people have it worse than me, so I should shape up and be grateful" attitude? Friend, this is still a comparison! Pointing out that other people are walking through a worse situation is no healthier than trying to make yourself a martyr.

We look around us, and we compare, but God uses His own lens to look at our individual situations. He knows that we need individual care and provision. The Gospel of Luke gives us the following example of Jesus addressing individual needs:

> "Then Jesus told them this parable: "Suppose one of you has a hundred sheep and loses one of them. Doesn't he leave the ninety-nine in the open country and go after the lost sheep until he finds it? And when he finds it, he joyfully puts it on his shoulders and goes home. Then he calls his friends and neighbors together and says, 'Rejoice with me; I have found my lost sheep.' I tell you that in the same way there will be more rejoicing over one sinner who repents than over ninety-nine righteous persons who do not need to repent."
>
> – Luke 15:3-7

The truth is that Jesus loves each of us, but that does not mean we all have the same experiences. We do not need to wear ourselves out comparing ourselves and our situations to others. We can, however, rest in the knowledge that He knows us individually, and He will give us what we need. He will even chase after us if we wander off. Did you notice in the Scripture passage above that Jesus is not grumbling about the sheep that wandered away and comparing it to the sheep who were smart enough not to get lost? Likewise, He does not keep a score for our bad attitudes and moments of doubt.

We are all unique individuals facing our own set of challenges, and God equips us exactly as He sees fit. Rather than comparing yourself to others, spend time checking in with the Lord and with the feelings in your own heart. God is not comparing you to others and assessing your worthiness. He loves you as is. Full stop. His love is endless and infinite and does not need to be divided up like Thanksgiving pie or a piece of Hubba Bubba®. This journey is not about what you do compared to someone else, but rather, it is about allowing the Holy Spirit to guide you as you work for the glory of the Lord. He has placed you in this role. He knows you can do what is needed as you rely on Him, and that is the truth.

PERSPECTIVE SHIFT:

The demands and challenges we face as caregivers are ongoing, but we can reframe our experience by shifting our perspective. By learning to view our situation through the lens of God's Word and by leaning into the Truth it provides, we can begin to move from feeling fearful to hopeful, from embattled to empowered in Christ, and from unseen to unconditionally loved.

SACRIFICE: What have you missed out on while you were busy battling the comparison trap?

HOPE: How does it feel to know that Jesus isn't comparing you to others? Does this help you move forward?

INTERVENTION: Pay attention to your own thoughts. When you find yourself feeling like you must earn your worth, replace that with the truth that Christ has saved and redeemed you.

FOLLOW-UP: Evaluate your situation. Has resting in the Truth helped you to change your inner voice?

TRUST: *Heavenly Father, instill in us a deep knowledge of Your abiding love. Lord, we pray that You will help us to let go of the idea that we must earn Your love. Help us trust that we are Yours and cannot be snatched out of Your hand. Be with us as we move forward in this journey, and help us to know You more each day.*

Amen.

CHAPTER 4

HOLDING ON AND LETTING GO

"Never be afraid to trust an unknown future to a known God."
— Corrie Ten Boom[1]

$\mathscr{H}$ ave you noticed that we live in a culture that values, even idolizes, self-sufficiency? We are a buckle-down, pull-yourself-up-by-the-bootstraps, get-it-done kind of people. This can be useful in some areas of our lives but not in others. For example, when my kids were little, I remember being so happy for a little extra sleep when my first child learned to pour cereal and turn on Saturday morning cartoons. It's easy for us to celebrate our children as they grow and learn and become competent in new skills, and rightfully so, but is it possible that the independence that we prize can become too much of a good thing? If we aren't careful, this can happen when we over-prioritize self-dependence over our dependence on God.

LIE #4: IT'S NOT SAFE TO "JUST TRUST GOD"

Who is the most trustworthy and dependable person you know? Think about it for a moment and pay attention to the first person who comes to mind. Okay, are you ready to answer? Be honest, my friend. Did you say, "Me"?

I'll admit that I struggle with delegation, even with the small stuff. Why? Because deep down, I worry that other people won't do things the way I think they should be done. I'm that woman who is tempted to reload the dishwasher the "right" way after someone else cleans up, and even if I don't actually rearrange the dirty dishes, I at least think about it. I have to make a conscious effort to leave it alone. Caregivers, especially those of us who lack support, can easily fall into the trap of believing that we are the only ones who will do things correctly. We become accustomed to doing things on our own, without outside counsel or commentary. Experience teaches us that we are the reliable ones. We are the ones who can be counted on, and as reliable as we may be, God calls us to trust in Him, not in ourselves alone.

Have you ever stopped and given serious thought to the topic of trust? What comes immediately to mind? For many of us, God is not first on the list. The Bible mentions trust in God or some variation thereof 134 times.[2] The repetition of a theme in Scripture underlines the importance of the topic. If God tells us something repeatedly, He has reason for doing so. The following verse about trust passed by me the first few times I read it:

> *"Some trust in chariots and some in horses, but we trust in the name of the Lord our God."*
>
> —Psalm 20:7

This verse seemed out of date and not applicable to my life. I don't even have chariots and horses. Surely, I don't trust in them – do I? As it turned out, I absolutely did; I just called them by different names. My horses and chariots are the diagnosis, the treatment plan, or a timeline for this season in life. I want the medication to fix things now. I want worldly trouble to disappear and for things to be "fair." And I want to trust in the Lord, really, but I often fail.

I was mired in self-dependence and, frankly, discouraged with the results I was producing. I was looking at things through my own eyes – using a worldly measuring stick to size up the horses and chariots. It can be especially frustrating to make this mistake during seasons of waiting, when we struggle to place all our trust in God. We wait on test results; we wait for physical therapy to be helpful, and we wait for the medications to come into full therapeutic effect. We wait, and we become ever more impatient. Picture an hourglass just as it gets turned over: all the sand is at the top, but ever so slowly is pouring into the bottom of the glass. Does that sand represent our faith and our patience? We start out trusting God and feeling strong in our faith, but as the hours tick by and we don't get good news or see physical improvement, our doubt starts to elbow our faith out of the way. Doubt leads to fear, and in these moments, I find myself wondering, is it really safe to just trust God? We want a sense of control. Why? Because we trust ourselves above all else. We place our faith in the medical advice and the treatment regimens, and sometimes, we learn that a good horse just won't do.

Psalm 20:7 teaches us to trust in God, not our inner strength or our abilities. Why do we struggle with this? Many of us have a hard time because we cannot measure God, nor do we understand the big picture. His ways are not our ways. This is part of our ongoing walk of discipleship: we live in the now and the not yet. We experience the saving grace of Christ while still living in a broken world. Many of us have given our hearts to others in the past, and we have been dependent on them in a way that comes naturally but is not the way we should anchor our identities. Our true identities are as believers in Christ Jesus, but we can misplace that from time to time. We learn hard lessons about disappointment and rejection because even the people that we love most in this world are still imperfect human beings who are incapable of being our everything. They make mistakes, they occasionally disappoint us – sometimes they even get sick – and eventually might die, breaking our hearts in the process.

The Lord knows that we struggle to trust things that we cannot see, and the Gospel of John gives us an example of this with the story of the disciple Thomas. Even one of Jesus' chosen 12 had trouble trusting without seeing. The other disciples told Thomas that they had seen Jesus after His death and resurrection:

> "Now Thomas (also known as Didymus), one of the Twelve, was not with the disciples when Jesus came. So the other disciples told him, 'We have seen the Lord!' But he said to them, 'Unless I see the nail marks in his hands and put my finger where the nails were, and put my hand into his side, I will not believe.' A week later his disciples were in the house again, and Thomas was with them. Though the doors were locked, Jesus came and stood among them and said, 'Peace be with you!' Then he said to Thomas, 'Put your finger here, see my hands. Reach out your hand and put it into my side. Stop doubting and believe.'"
>
> – John 20:24-27

We do not have an accurate earthly comparison for God's love, forgiveness, compassion, or patience, but we see shadows of it. Unlike Thomas, we don't get to put our hands on the wounds of Jesus, but we can learn from this interaction. Jesus meets Thomas where he is – right in the middle of his doubt. Jesus gave Thomas exactly what he needed: reassurance. My friend, Jesus reassures us, also. He gives us small examples for something so big that we struggle to fully comprehend it: the self-sacrificing love of a mother for her child, the grown child who drives her mom to chemotherapy appointments, the first responder who rushes into danger to save strangers, a loyal wife who holds her husband's hands as he crosses from this world into the next. The small shadows of God's love are all around us, and each one is an invitation for us to remember the truth. God loves us, values us, and wants us to draw near Him.

We like to feel safe, and sometimes, we forget that trusting in God instead of ourselves is the surest way to shelter in the storms. Who among us hasn't tried to guard against the pain that we see coming? We are inclined to try to protect ourselves, although we often turn towards ourselves instead of the Lord. Many of us are wired to act in a crisis, and I'm in that category. Keeping occupied creates a sense of control. Busy hands help to quiet my racing thoughts, my fears, and the unsettling what-if questions. Shifting my focus off the crisis and onto the peripheral duties of caregiving allows me to harden my heart. I can concentrate on the tasks in front of me and avoid dealing with the terrifying care decisions that I'm not prepared to make.

The first chapter of the Gospel of Luke tells us about the priest Zechariah, the father of John the Baptist. Zechariah was a good man, but he made mistakes, just like we all do. Zechariah relied on his own knowledge and experience rather than trusting God by accepting what God's angel told him. Let's take a look together:

> "Once when Zechariah's division was on duty and he was serving as priest before God, he was chosen by lot, according to the custom of the priesthood, to go into the temple of the Lord and burn incense. And when the time for the burning of the incense came, all the assembled worshipers were praying outside.

> Then an angel of the Lord appeared to him, standing at the right side of the altar of incense. When Zechariah saw him, he was startled, and gripped with fear. But the angel said to him:

> 'Do not be afraid, Zechariah; your prayer has been heard. Your wife Elizabeth will bear you a son, and you are to call him John. He will be a joy and delight to you,

*and many will rejoice because of his birth, for he will be
great in the sight of the Lord. He is never to take wine or
any fermented drink, and he will be filled with the Holy
Spirit even before he is born. He will bring back many of
the people of Israel to the Lord their God. And he will go
on before the Lord, in the spirit and the power of Elijah,
to turn the hearts of the parents to their children and
the disobedient to the wisdom of the righteous- to make
ready a people prepared for the Lord.'"*

Zechariah should have rejoiced with this news, but instead,
he hardened his heart against possible disappointment.

Zechariah asked the angel,

*"'How can I be sure of this? I am an old man and my
wife is well along in years.' The angel said to him, 'I am
Gabriel. I stand in the presence of God, and I have been
sent to speak to you and to tell you this good news. And
now you will be silent and not able to speak until this
happens, because you did not believe my words, which
will come true at their appointed time.'"*

– Luke 1:8-20

I'm from the South, and this passage brings to mind the
phrase people use when they hear something that's hard to
believe: "Well, shut my mouth!" I think it's safe to assume
Zechariah wasn't so flippant with an angel, but nonetheless,
Gabriel *did* shut Zechariah's mouth. Because of his disbelief, he
was mute until his son was born.

Why are we afraid to *fully* trust God? For starters, we are
human, and we fail. Deep down, we want to feel safe and
protected, so sometimes we build walls. Much like the people of
ancient cities constructed walls to keep out invaders, we build
walls around our hearts to keep out pain and disappointment.
Sometimes, it's intentional and proactive, but sometimes, it's

reactive to the hurts that we've experienced. We try to protect ourselves, but God calls us to soften our hearts instead. Ezekiel 36:26 says:

> "I will give you a new heart and put a new spirit in you;
> I will remove from you your heart of stone and give you
> a heart of flesh."

Oh, to have a heart of flesh would be... terrifying. Here's my struggle: hearts of flesh are easily injured, while hearts of stone can feel like impenetrable fortresses. It's no surprise when we are so easily tempted to build walls around our hearts. One by one, we stack our hurts, injustices, and insecurities like expert masons placing stones. We build nice, strong walls around our hearts, and we think we are secure, but what we really are is hard-hearted. Self-dependence can lead to relying on ourselves instead of the goodness of the Lord. Our faith calls us to have hearts of flesh, not hearts of stone, which is challenging because we live with very real pain in a broken world. Pain and grief come in many forms, and whether they sneak in silently during the night, or beat down our doors with noise and fanfare, our response is often to steel ourselves. We try to stiffen up and depend on our own strength, which will never be enough.

Tearing down walls is hard work. Sometimes, removing the first stone is easy. It's exciting to make a change and do something that will bring you closer to the Lord. But the reality is that it takes a long time to build big, strong walls around our hearts, and it takes a long time to dismantle them. Have you ever watched one of those HGTV shows that starts with an ugly or dysfunctional house and transforms it into a beautiful and effective use of space? The happy homeowner smiles as she swings the mallet and makes the first hole in the drywall. What the episode probably doesn't showcase is most of the work thereafter. Swinging a mallet and changing the structure of a house is hard work. I'm guessing that any of you who have survived a home remodeling project can attest to the challenges that go on behind the scenes: the arguments with your spouse, the stress caused by budget overruns, and the plain exhaustion that comes from working so hard. We might be wondering to ourselves, "Why on earth did I start this project?" Tearing down the walls we build around our hearts is every bit as difficult as literal demolition, and we will hit roadblocks along the way.

We find it difficult to break down our barriers because we are still learning that we don't work alone. God is the master builder, and we need to rely on Him to eliminate our protective walls and build a heart of flesh. As we work to dismantle our walls, we discover that we don't know how to put ourselves back together. Try as we might, we cannot make our hearts whole without Jesus. He can take our shards of stone and make them flesh. One way to move forward with a softened heart is to practice gratitude towards the Lord. Are your eyes open to His presence in your life? Try being mindful of your circumstances and write down some ways in which the Lord has blessed you, provided for you, or answered your prayers. Worship is another way to practice giving our hearts to God. Weekly worship services are a wonderful way to do this, but we can also worship with music at any time. Lifting our voices in praise, especially during a dark time, shows our desire to trust in Him.

Friend, I know it can feel scary, but the safest thing you can do is to entrust your entire self to the Lord. We try so hard to hold onto control, to color within the lines, and to make our hours predictable in a misguided attempt to make things easier. I implore you: stop fighting so hard to protect your heart and surrender it to the One who will make it whole. I know the challenge of loosening the grip of our hands and letting go of self-dependence, but I also know the reward that comes from doing just that. Let go of your fear and grab hold of the Lord, who will never forsake you. The rock-solid truth is that trusting God is the safest thing you could ever do.

PERSPECTIVE SHIFT:

The demands and challenges we face as caregivers are ongoing, but we can reframe our experience by shifting our perspective. By learning to view our situation through the lens of God's Word and by leaning into the Truth it provides, we can begin to move from feeling fearful to hopeful, from embattled to empowered in Christ, and from unseen to unconditionally loved.

SACRIFICE: What have your strong walls kept out of your heart?

HOPE: What would it feel like to fully surrender to the Lord?

INTERVENTION: Write your own prayer asking God to accept your complete surrender to His loving care.

FOLLOW-UP: What emotions did you experience as you wrote your prayer?

TRUST: *Heavenly Father, here in our earthly lives, trust is usually earned. We guard our hearts and are afraid to give up control in our lives. Help us, we pray, to stop mapping the road by ourselves. We need You, Lord. We trust You. We surrender.*

Amen.

PART 3

DISCERN NEEDS

"Do not be conformed to this world, but be transformed by the renewal of your mind, that by testing you may discern what is the will of God, what is good and acceptable and perfect."
— **Romans 12:2, ESV**

CHAPTER 5

BEYOND THE SUPERWOMAN SYNDROME

"There is a part of Wonder Woman inside me and inside every woman, kind of that secret self that women share. We are all caretakers, giving birth, caring for our children and companions and loved ones."
— Lynda Carter[1]

*M*y family sat in stunned silence as we processed the news we had just received from the ER doctor. My mother-in-law had suffered a major stroke, and she was no longer capable of making her own medical decisions, so now we had to do it for her. The weight of our new responsibility landed squarely on our shoulders, and oh my goodness – was it ever heavy! We faced a life-or-death decision.

It seemed like there should be an obvious answer about the best way to take care of her, but if there was, we couldn't see it through our tears. Guilt marched itself right into that waiting room and tapped its fingers on the table — impatiently waiting for someone to come to a decision. I remember feeling lost and confused in that moment, as if I had studied for an exam and then forgot everything as the test paper sat in front of me on the desk. For the life of me, I couldn't wrap my head around the concept that we didn't know the next right step to take.

I was so focused on the medical decision before us that I failed to realize that the next right step for me was to take this problem to the Lord. I was still operating out of a place of fear and self-dependence, and I bought into the lie that I — myself alone — should know what my mother-in-law needed.

LIE #5: I SHOULD KNOW WHAT EVERYONE NEEDS

The question was: what should we do? One option was to send her into the operating room and try to repair the bleed, but her odds of surviving that surgery were not good. The other option was to forego surgery – in which case, her odds of meaningful recovery were slim. We sat in that waiting room in between the proverbial rock and a hard place and tried to reason things out. To make things more complicated, we were receiving conflicting advice from doctors. It seemed that I wasn't the only one struggling to figure out what she needed.

Have you perhaps been called upon to make decisions that you felt unqualified to make? Maybe, like me, your inclination was to lean on your own understanding, but instead of answers, you only found more questions. As I was faced with the monumental task of selecting a treatment option, I began to understand that I needed to discern, not just decide. I needed to take the information at hand with the Truth of God and ask Him to help us.

As caregivers, we often face making decisions for our loved ones. We might decide which cereal to purchase for Dad at the grocery store, select the right medical specialist, or even make the call that it's time for hospice care. I often felt overloaded during this season of my life as I struggled to maintain clarity when faced with making seemingly endless decisions. When faced with so many demands on both our time and our spirits, how do we begin to decide what is true and right? How do we prioritize things?

The truth is that God is the only one who always knows what we need, and He always provides. Sometimes, the Lord provides directly; sometimes, His provision comes through people or systems He has placed around us. The book of Ruth is a good example of God's provision through various means. Boaz is a kinsman-redeemer for Naomi's family, which means that he could be called upon to redeem the land (buy it back for the family), avenge a death, or even provide an heir..[2] Let's look at this passage where Naomi instructs Ruth to approach Boaz privately and ask for his protection. Here, Naomi gives some instructions that seem strange to our modern sensibilities:

> "One day Ruth's mother-in-law Naomi said to her, 'My daughter, I must find a home for you, where you will be well provided for. Now Boaz, with whose women you have worked, is a relative of ours. Tonight he will be winnowing barley on the threshing floor. Wash, put on perfume, and put on your best clothes. Then go down to the threshing floor, but don't let him know you are there until he has finished eating and drinking. When he lies down, note the place where he is lying. Then go and uncover his feet and lie down. He will tell you what to do.'"
>
> – Ruth 3:1-4

This may sound like Naomi is sending Ruth to seduce Boaz, but that's not supported by the text. In Jewish custom at this time, a husband would cover his bride with the end of his prayer shawl, symbolically demonstrating that she is under his protection.[3] The kinsman-redeemer had the freedom to accept or deny a request, so asking for protection is not without risk of rejection. Ruth, ever trusting and loyal, does as Naomi has instructed:

> "When Boaz had finished eating and drinking and was in good spirits, he went over to lie down at the far end of the grain pile. Ruth approached quietly, uncovered his feet and lay down. In the middle of the night something startled the man; he turned – and there was a woman lying at his feet! 'Who are you?' he asked. 'I am your servant Ruth,' she said. 'Spread the corner of your garment over me, since you are a guardian-redeemer of our family.'"
>
> – Ruth 3:7-9

In this passage, Naomi, Ruth, and Boaz all walk through a process of discernment. Naomi understood the reality of the times she lived in – Ruth needed a husband and a protector. Ruth knew that Naomi was trustworthy and looking out for her best interests. Boaz had observed Ruth's character as she spent time working in his fields, and he believed her to be an honorable woman. Guided by God, they used the information at hand to inform their decisions.

We, too, should use discernment as we strive to find the best way forward through our caregiving journeys. When we begin with prayer, we not only tell God what we need, but we actively seek His guidance. Like Ruth, we also need to be willing to work hard. She toiled in the field to feed herself and Naomi. God provided, but Ruth had to put in her own effort. We also should remember to keep kindness and compassion at the heart of our decision-making.

Our loved ones depend on us to recognize and meet their needs. Sometimes, the needs are obvious, but oftentimes, we may need to examine the situation more closely. It's important to remember that while some of our loved ones are great at advocating for themselves, others don't speak up – they are afraid of becoming a burden. That's right – the "B" word – for many people, becoming a burden is one of their biggest fears.

Many of us don't like asking for help, and that naturally includes our loved ones who are now in need of our care. They might sacrifice social relationships or other activities due to transportation or mobility issues, preferring to keep quiet instead of asking for our help. We should be on the lookout for this type of disengagement, as social isolation can lead to a host of other problems.[4] How can we tell if our loved ones are socially connected? We can start by observing. Does Mom have visitors at least once a week? Does Dad still attend worship services? Has your husband given up his occasional golf outing? Another way to gather information is to ask engaging questions, but be careful not to interrogate. We might inquire to Mom, "What happened today that was interesting?"

In addition to watching out for social isolation, we should assess the other things our care recipient is doing or has given up doing. Physical difficulties, such as declining eyesight, can make it challenging to continue long-loved hobbies. Artists can lose the ability to distinguish brush strokes of paint on a canvas. Chefs may have a hard time reading the measuring spoons. Arthritis, a common ailment of old age, often robs people of fine motor function. A beautiful garden becomes an overgrown eyesore, and the woman who was known for her green thumb is now embarrassed about her yard. Our loved ones understand the natural physical deterioration and inconveniences that come with aging, but what they fear is a lack of independence. And to be honest, we fear it too.

I remember feeling frustrated when my husband, after working all day, would have to make a quick exit from the dinner table to go deal with the day's crisis. My father-in-law, Doyle, had Alzheimer's Disease, and while my mother-in-law handled most caregiving, Doyle was a bit of a handful. Sometimes she needed reinforcements – which I totally understood – but at the same time, why did it always have to be at dinner time? By this point in my day, I was exhausted, and I felt cheated when my husband had to leave almost as soon as he arrived home.

My father-in-law's increasing need for care had a ripple effect on the entire family. It's possible that you have experienced something similar, especially if you belong to the sandwich generation – taking care of aging parents while you are still raising your children. Many of us are "sandwiched" in our caregiving journeys. We find ourselves trying to sort out our priorities. Who should come first – our children or our parents? Facing competing demands as multiple people needed my time and energy, I had to come to peace with the fact that sometimes discernment means making hard choices and allowing someone to be unhappy. There may be situations in which the right answer is that only one person gets what she needs in a given moment, as we are tasked with prioritizing multiple needs.

As a nurse, I was taught to start any assessments with the ABCs: airway, breathing, circulation. In emergencies, we must prioritize the life-sustaining things first. For example, I'm not going to worry about a potential broken wrist if my patient is in cardiac arrest. This can be helpful for caregivers when we are considering the physical welfare of our loved ones. We can also use an ABC process for prioritizing emotional or spiritual needs and for figuring out how to best divide our time between our loved ones.

A: Assess and acknowledge the situation

Take in the information at hand. If Mom, a recovering stroke patient, is groaning and grimacing, that is a signal to look for something causing physical pain. If she is crying, check for physical pain, but be aware that it might be related to an unmet emotional need.

B: Biblically sound encouragement

We all need to be encouraged, and the best way to do this is by remaining in Truth. Sometimes, we offer encouragement with uplifting words, but sometimes, we offer it with our presence and our shared tears. Sometimes, we just don't have the right words. What do you say to the best friend faced with a cancer diagnosis? How can you encourage the mom whose child has been critically injured? It's easy to shy away from hard situations. Instead of turning a blind eye, we can look to God's Word for guidance. Love one another.

C: Christ-like care for yourself and others

What would Jesus do? I'm not advising you to get a WWJD rubber bracelet. I am suggesting that you stop and ask yourself: if Jesus were here in person, what would He do? How would He care for my loved one? How would He comfort her? How would He help me? We cannot measure up to Jesus, but He is our Redeemer and our ultimate example.

Let's face it: we are all just humans trying to make our way through this life. It's impossible for us to know what everyone around us needs. Friend, you will feel so much better once you let go of those unrealistic expectations of perfectly providing all things to all people. Throw those harmful thoughts out the window – they are only holding you back and making you feel guilty for not being Superwoman. Instead of looking to our own unrealistic expectations, let's instead recognize that God alone knows what everyone needs, and He doesn't need you trying to do His job. Find contentment not in knowing everything but in knowing the Truth. Stand in the comfort of His protection, His knowledge, and His wisdom as you let go of the lie that you are supposed to know what everyone needs. God knows what they need, and the truth is that He knows what you need, too, my friend. You need Him.

PERSPECTIVE SHIFT:

The demands and challenges we face as caregivers are ongoing, but we can reframe our experience by shifting our perspective. By learning to view our situation through the lens of God's Word and by leaning into the Truth it provides, we can begin to move from feeling fearful to hopeful, from embattled to empowered in Christ, and from unseen to unconditionally loved.

SACRIFICE: What emotions have you experienced when you didn't anticipate someone's needs?

HOPE: How can setting reasonable expectations help you as you move forward? Consider what makes sense for your situation in terms of time management, task expectations, financial commitments, and emotional boundaries.

INTERVENTION: Employ the stop, look, and listen tactic. Use interactions with your loved ones as a chance to gather valuable information about what they might need.

FOLLOW-UP: Has the stop, look, and listen tactic enabled you to better understand the needs of your loved one?

TRUST: *Lord, only You know what everyone needs. Help us to trust in that truth. Likewise, walk with us, we pray, as we strive to give the best possible care to Your children. Bless us with wisdom and endurance so that we may care for others as You care for us.*

Amen.

CHAPTER 6

SELF-CARE IN SEASONS OF SACRIFICE

"Remember always that you not only have the right to be an individual, you have an obligation to be one."
– Eleanor Roosevelt[1]

*H*ave you ever had one of those moments when you realize all your sacrifices have been worth it? Perhaps, like me, you had a moment of clarity and assurance when you knew that the things you gave up paled in comparison to the value of taking care of another person. My young son snuggled up on my lap and pronounced, "I love you, Mommy!" My heart warmed with the feeling of a job well done, but it was a fleeting moment as he added, "I love you more than a grilled cheese sandwich." And there it was: my ranking – just above lunch. I'll admit that my feelings of deflation soon turned to frustration as I sat with the thoughts that my actions, and therefore my very self, didn't matter much. I didn't expect my needs to come in front of everyone else, but I've got to be honest here: getting compared to two pieces of white bread and a Kraft® slice was a bit disheartening. This moment, and others like it, led me to grow in my belief in a lie: that what I needed didn't matter anymore.

LIE #6: WHAT I NEED DOESN'T MATTER ANYMORE

I didn't intend to give up my Monday night Bible study. It started with a singular absence, a one-off, and it was not a big deal. As the next weekly meeting rolled around, I didn't think much of it when, once again, I had my hands full taking care of a sick kid. By the third Monday, I was feeling a bit out of sorts as I found myself not at Bible study but rather in the ER – not exactly what one would call an upgrade.

Bible study was the last thing on my mind as we were subsequently admitted to the hospital, and the only thing I felt like I needed was for my son to get better. He couldn't stop vomiting and was right on the border of needing a feeding tube. To make things worse, none of the doctors could identify a cause for his symptoms. We remained in the hospital for a week, and by that point, I was sleep-deprived, anxious, angry, and exhausted – but mostly, I was his mom. To my mind, this meant that I had to be *the one*: the one who engages with the doctors, the one to hold his hand and comfort him when he's scared and in pain, the one who coaxed him to keep taking in fluids, even when he didn't want to eat or drink.

His illness dragged on, and I wearily continued being *the one*. I felt frayed around the edges and well on my way to breaking. I felt like there was no end in sight, and I didn't have any idea how I was supposed to keep going. My friend, if this sounds familiar, perhaps you, too, have experienced the physical and emotional exhaustion that can strike when we forget to take care of ourselves. Your needs are still important even as you find yourself overwhelmed with taking care of someone else. We've all heard the flight attendant's safety speech:

It's unlikely but if cabin pressure changes, the panels above your seat will open revealing oxygen masks. If this happens, reach up and pull the mask towards you until the tube is fully extended. Place the mask over your nose and mouth. Slip the elastic strap over your head and adjust the mask if necessary. Breathe normally and note that oxygen is flowing; so, don't worry if the bag doesn't inflate. Be sure to adjust your own mask before helping others.[2]

As a caregiver, you may be wired to help others before yourself, but it is imperative that you put on your oxygen mask first! You cannot take care of someone else if you aren't physically and emotionally equipped to do so. Our loved ones are depending on us – not only to take care of them, but to take care of ourselves as well.

Nancy's Story:

Nancy takes care of her husband, Robert, who suffers from Alzheimer's Disease. She started putting off routine medical appointments for herself when Robert's behavior became difficult to handle. Patients with Alzheimer's or other dementia-related diseases often exhibit challenging behavior caused by their disorder. They may do things such as yell, swear, run away, or even act out physically. As Robert's health declined, Nancy continued missing appointments that she should have been keeping for herself as her husband's needs overshadowed her own.

One activity that Nancy never let up on was cleaning the house, but even this became difficult. One afternoon, Robert didn't understand not to walk across the freshly waxed hardwood floor. Nancy repeatedly instructed him not to walk on the slick floor, afraid he would fall and get hurt, but Robert forgot her instructions as soon as he heard them. As he approached once more, Nancy put up her hands and exclaimed, "Wait!" Things changed in the blink of an eye as Robert, who had never been a violent man, pushed his wife. Nancy went flying and broke her fall with her hand. The pain was immediate and severe, and she knew at that moment that her wrist was broken.

Now, Nancy was facing both a physical problem and a caregiving problem. Robert required help to do many things, and Nancy feared what could happen if she was unable to help him. Nancy was honest about these challenges when she had her appointment with the orthopedist, who recommended surgery to pin the bones and get optimal healing. She declined the surgery because she couldn't be out of commission for the healing time it required. Nancy worked together with her doctor on a compromise, and she ended up casting the broken bone, having decided that she would just have to live with the risk that it wouldn't heal properly.

Unfortunately, Nancy's story is not unique. So often, caregivers feel isolated and are doing their best just to keep their heads above water. We sacrifice our financial security, our physical health, and even our emotional well-being – we forget to put our oxygen masks on first. We need to recognize that it is important to take care of ourselves while also understanding that self-care might look different for a while. We wouldn't want our loved one to skip medical appointments or to have poor nutrition and a sedentary lifestyle, but we struggle to recognize our own needs. Caregivers commonly report suffering from lack of sleep, over or under-eating, delayed routine medical care, and a decrease in opportunities to socialize.[3] We often give these things up because we feel as if there is no other choice. Sometimes, we do have to put our needs on hold during a particularly busy or stressful time, but we should also remember that the Lord loves us, cares for us, and wants us to be taken care of, too. If you have found that you are putting yourself last, please know that what you need still matters. You might need to shift your needs to the back burner for a little while, but don't turn the stove off.

As women, we are often expected to put the needs of others before our own, and it's an easy slide from there to a place where we put ourselves last. As simple as it might sound, we need to make time to take a shower every day, eat our meals on a regular schedule, and at least try to go to bed on time. Self-care comes in a wide variety of shapes and sizes, and I understand from personal experience that it can be hard to take care of yourself when it feels like the weight of the world is on your shoulders. It may feel like you don't have a spare minute out of the day to devote to self-care. Try listening to your favorite music while feeding your mom or work on a crossword puzzle while you wait with your husband to be summoned from the waiting room to the exam room. Find what works for you and try to add it into your day.

I imagine there wasn't a big focus on self-care during ancient times. Life then was, in many ways, much harsher than it is today. The Israelites lived lives of labor tempered with periods of rest, but they also faced the realities of their time, and they worked as though their survival depended on it – because it did. Ruth was an extremely hard worker and she toiled in the fields gathering food. Boaz, the landowner, saw Ruth and asked the overseer of the harvesters who she was.

> "The overseer replied, 'She is the Moabite who came back from Moab with Naomi. She said, 'Please let me glean and gather among the sheaves behind the harvesters.' She came into the field and has remained here from morning till now, except for a short rest in the shelter.'"
>
> – Ruth 2:6-7

Ruth shows us here that she understood the consequences of working and still took time for a short break. Harvesting crops is physically demanding work. She labored without complaint, but she also understood the need for rest. As caregivers, we can look to Ruth as an example. While we are not in the field harvesting crops, the work we do is life-giving to our loved ones. We need to remember to take a short rest in the shelter, even on the hardest of days.

My friend, you are a beloved daughter of the King, an heir in Christ, and you are precious in the sight of the Lord. You matter, and what you need matters because He says so. God Himself created you – you are fearfully and wonderfully made – and He wants you to be taken care of. Scripture tells us, "Don't you know that you yourselves are God's temple and that God's Spirit dwells in your midst?" (1 Corinthians 3:16) The truth is that you are worth taking care of, what you need does matter, and God will always take care of you no matter what season you are walking through.

PERSPECTIVE SHIFT:

The demands and challenges we face as caregivers are ongoing, but we can reframe our experience by shifting our perspective. By learning to view our situation through the lens of God's Word and by leaning into the Truth it provides, we can begin to move from feeling fearful to hopeful, from embattled to empowered in Christ, and from unseen to unconditionally loved.

SACRIFICE: What self-care activities have you skipped while caregiving for someone else?

HOPE: What would you like to be able to add back into your self-care regimen?

INTERVENTION: Identify one or two tasks that you could delegate to free up some time for yourself.

FOLLOW-UP: What activity were you able to indulge in by delegating caregiving duties?

TRUST: *Heavenly Father, help us to remember that we are also Your precious children and to trust that You want to help take care of us. Lead us to opportunities that will help us to take care of ourselves – bodies and souls – for we are Yours.*

Amen.

PART 4

ENGAGE IN CAREGIVING

"The King will reply, 'Truly I tell you, whatever you did for one of the least of these brothers and sisters of mine, you did for me.'"
– Matthew 25:40

CHAPTER 7

ADAPTING THROUGH THE OVERWHELM

"If you want a thing done well, do it yourself."
—Napoleon Bonaparte[1]

didn't sign up for this. My stomach tightened into a knot every time my phone chimed with a text message that could signal the next demand on my time. I was a woman trying to keep all the balls in the air and let's face it; I don't even know how to juggle! My father-in-law had Alzheimer's Disease, my mother-in-law was recovering from a major stroke, and my grandmother was dealing with the typical issues of an 80+-year-old aging body. Meanwhile, my illness-prone kids were seemingly determined to catch every virus known to man. I felt like I was struggling to catch my breath as I ran from one crisis to another.

I was weighed down with not only the physical tasks but also the emotional load of feeling like I had to do everything by myself. In hindsight, I can see that there were plenty of people who would have stepped up to support me had I only been brave enough to ask for help. I had somehow internalized the belief that a good mother, a good daughter-in-law, or a good granddaughter shouldn't need to ask for help. I believed that my love for them should have been enough to keep me going. I was snared by the lie that I should be able to do it all myself.

LIE #7: I MUST DO IT ALL MYSELF

Ping. Ping. Ping. The text messages on my phone came at rapid-fire speed. I whipped my phone out of my purse and quickly scanned the incoming messages. I was mentally prioritizing each move as I continued working to get my children ready for school. I took a deep breath and told myself, "It's okay, you've got this." I'm an organized person, and I reasoned that with enough logic, creative scheduling, and sheer willpower, I could get everything done. It seems laughable now that I bought into the lie that I needed to do it all, much less that I needed to do it by myself. My intentions were good, but my execution needed some work.

I'm a calendar-loving, list-making, type-A oldest child, but here's the thing: caregiving responsibilities are bigger than any calendar. They are bigger than both my good intentions and my ability to completely plan for them. Exhaustion eventually led me to the conclusion that I needed to get real about the situation I was facing.

Looking back, I wondered: why on earth did I ever think I could manage this caregiving gig by myself? I didn't even know what was involved, and that's one of the tricky things about caregiving. It's not a course that's offered in school – most of us just have to figure it out. Trust me, friend, I went to nursing school, and managing how to take care of a family member isn't on the course list. It's hard to get your arms around taking care of someone in a nonprofessional setting. Caregiving is both one herculean task and a million little things all at the same time. Not only that, but the requirements for caregiving frequently change as illnesses progress, injuries heal, or new diagnoses are added to the mix. Adaptability is important, but it can be hard to think strategically when we are struggling to put one foot in front of the other.

Sometimes, we can't even see the big picture, and the only thing we can do is take that one next step in our caregiving journey. In fact, the Bible gives us a beautiful example of this in the book of Ruth. Much like how our caregiving journeys don't always follow a straight line, we will be exploring the book of Ruth as it relates to our caregiving topic, which will not always be in chronological order. Naomi, Ruth's mother-in-law, learns that the famine in Judah has ended. Naomi was vulnerable without a male protector. Still grieving the loss of her husband and sons, she decides to return home to Bethlehem. Naomi tells her daughters-in-law that she intends to go home. They both offer to accompany her. Instead of accepting their offer, she urges them to return to the homes of their mothers. She points out that she has nothing to offer them and says they should remarry and carry on. Orpah relents. Ruth, however, makes a different, life-changing decision.

> *"'Look,' said Naomi, 'your sister-in-law is going back to her people and her gods. Go back with her.' But Ruth replied, 'Don't urge me to leave you or turn back from you. Where you go I will go, and where you stay, I will stay. Your people will be my people and your God will be my God. Where you die I will die, and there I will be buried. May the Lord deal with me, be it ever so severely, if even death separates you and me.' When Naomi realized that Ruth was determined to go with her, she stopped urging her. So the two women went on until they came to Bethlehem..."*
>
> —Ruth 1:15-19

The first caregiving act that we see in this chapter is Ruth's decision to journey with Naomi. She, like many of us, knows that the road ahead is uncertain but likely difficult. Ruth has no reason to believe that good things await her in Bethlehem. She has no husband, money, or status. She is a Moabitess, an outsider among the Jewish community, and considered undesirable. Though the situation seems grim, Ruth acts, and with this one brave decision, she sets into motion a series of events that would surprise everyone.

Like Ruth, we begin our journeys with a decision. We choose to step up, give the care, and stand in the gap. Oftentimes, we will feel like we don't have a choice. We may be the only ones available to help, and without us, there seems to be no solution. It might be obvious to us that the right choice is to step into the role of a caregiver, even if we do so with trepidation and a heavy heart. Ruth isn't the only one who makes brave decisions. While we step forward with courage, we need to remember that we don't have to do this alone – Jesus will help us.

Caregiving typically draws to mind physical tasks, such as medication administration and housekeeping. Those things are important, and as caregivers, we will actively spend our time on them. A great deal of our caregiving duties revolve around these jobs. Often, a loved one will need help with Instrumental Activities of Daily Living (IADLs). These are things such as cooking, cleaning, laundry, transportation, and managing their finances and medications.[2] This can be the stage when we are most likely to mistakenly believe that we can, in fact, do this all by ourselves. Maybe Grandpa can't do his laundry right now because his arthritis is so bad that he can't hold the laundry basket, or perhaps you've noticed that financially responsible Grandma has stacks of unpaid bills scattered around the house. You aren't entirely sure, but you think your husband hasn't been taking his medications on a regular basis, although he insists that he has. These needs seem small, trifling even, and we tell ourselves it's manageable: "Of course, I can do some laundry for Grandpa. I'll automate all the bill paying to remove that burden from Grandma. Not a big deal. I'll get my husband one of those plastic day-of-the-week pill containers. Easy-peasy. I've got this."

There are a few things that can trip us up here. The first is that, for a while, we do have it all together. We are successfully relying on our own strength and our own power to manage our responsibilities, and then the adjusted situation becomes the new normal against which we measure change. It's so easy to believe we can handle it all when things start small and only grow an inch at a time. We do laundry, pay bills, and keep medicines on track without breaking a sweat, but life has a funny way of turning up the speed on the treadmill just as we find a comfortable pace.

There is a classic episode of the show *I Love Lucy*[3] that demonstrates this concept. Lucy and Ethel get jobs at a candy factory. The boss gives instructions on how they are supposed to wrap each candy in paper as it comes down the assembly line. The conveyor belt turns on, and Lucy and Ethel start wrapping the candies as instructed. They've got this! Then, as the speed of the conveyor belt increases, Lucy and Ethel work faster and faster. As candies start to travel past them without being wrapped, Ethel compensates by trying to eat the extra candies, and it's not long before she looks like a chipmunk with cheeks stuffed full to bursting. Lucy joins in the effort and grabs the extra candies and puts them in her pockets, in her hat, and eventually, even down the front of her shirt! Lucy and Ethel seem relieved when the boss comes back in and announces, "Fine. You're doing splendidly." They exhale with a sigh of relief just as the boss bellows to the people controlling the conveyor belt, "Speed it up a little!"

Like Lucy and Ethel, we probably don't feel like we're at risk of losing control when the conveyor belt is moving slowly. People don't usually drown in ankle-deep water. Typically, our responsibilities will add up over time. Our loved ones probably start out needing help with one or two IADLs. Then it turns into three or four and even more. Further declines in health might mean that you now need to help with Activities of Daily Living (ADLs), and this could be where you feel like the rubber really meets the road. ADLs tend to involve more hands-on and time-consuming care. Mom can no longer cook her own meals OR be responsible for feeding herself. Dad needs help getting dressed and undressed. Your sister is in a wheelchair and can't transfer herself from the chair to the bed. Your spouse needs help with toileting. Yes, toileting. That's the dreaded one, isn't it?

Let's take a minute because we need to get real about bodily functions and bodily fluids. Yes, we are going to talk about the "F" words: fluids, farts, and functions. They are a part of life, although the taboo part about which we've always been told to keep quiet. "F" words are the substances and behaviors that, while perfectly natural, are supposed to be kept hidden behind closed doors. Guess what? They won't always be behind closed doors. I'm not telling you this to discourage you but to acknowledge the reality that caregivers face every day. Adult diapers exist because there is a need for them. Illness and old age can bring some disheartening challenges with them: incontinence, lack of control over passing gas, difficulty eating or swallowing, and/or memory issues that cause socially unacceptable behavior.

Jane's Story

Jane experienced this "F" word reality while taking her father, who suffered from dementia, out for a ride in her new car. Larry didn't have many opportunities to get out of the house and was excited to go on an adventure with his daughter. She was driving him downtown on a Saturday to give him a tour of her office. Jane found herself going 70 miles per hour on the left lane of the highway when Larry announced that he needed to go to the bathroom. Right now. She signaled to get over and was going to get off at the first exit, but they didn't make it in time. Larry had diarrhea. The Depends® underwear caught some of it, but not all of it. Jane made it to the office building and took her dad into the bathroom, grateful that the only witness was a sympathetic security guard. She asked her dad to stay there while she darted across the street to the store to purchase new underwear and a pair of pants. Larry, thankfully, waited in the bathroom as instructed. Jane was able to clean him up and just throw away the soiled clothes. It wasn't the afternoon she had planned, and she had to kiss the new car smell goodbye.

Poop happens. Bathroom accidents are a fact of life for many people, and they can be tricky to deal with. Jane learned from her experience, though. She never again left the house without extra supplies, including a full set of clean clothes for her dad. Jane realized that despite her planning and careful organization, sometimes accidents happen. She was thankful for the kind security guard, and she was glad that her family commiserated with her rather than berating her for the misadventure of the afternoon.

The truth is that we should not realistically expect to tackle the enormous job of caregiving by ourselves. Supportive friends and family are nice to have, but really, we should be looking first to the Lord. Jesus Himself was subjected to numerous humiliations during His earthly life, and I think He has a heart for those of us walking through the broken places while taking care of one another.

Although it may feel like it at times, we are not called to do everything by ourselves. I know from personal experience that it can seem easier to stay quiet, do the job yourself, and not ask for help. Often, it can feel like teaching someone to take over a task is more trouble than just doing it yourself. We are overwhelmed, looking for the fastest and easiest path forward, but feelings of overwhelm can be one of the red flags that the Lord will throw out to get our attention. He calls us to quit playing the game of self-reliance and instead learn to adapt. Lean into the provision He puts around you, my friend, and trust the truth – that in all things, the Lord goes before you and paves the way.

PERSPECTIVE SHIFT:

The demands and challenges we face as caregivers are ongoing, but we can reframe our experience by shifting our perspective. By learning to view our situation through the lens of God's Word and by leaning into the Truth it provides, we can begin to move from feeling fearful to hopeful, from embattled to empowered in Christ, and from unseen to unconditionally loved.

SACRIFICE: What has changed in your daily routine since becoming a caregiver?

HOPE: How would it feel to know that you aren't supposed to do this all by yourself?

INTERVENTION: In the last chapter, we wrote down a few tasks we could delegate. Now, identify one or two people you trust enough to ask for help – and then reach out to them.

FOLLOW-UP: Did anyone step up to help you? List them in your journal..

TRUST: *Dear Lord, it is exhausting to try and shoulder the responsibilities of caregiving by ourselves. We are weary. We are overwhelmed. We are in desperate need of Your strength. Please be with us and help us remember that we are never alone. We trust that You are with us always.*

Amen.

CHAPTER 8

THE POWER OF ONE MORE STEP

"If you're going through hell, keep going."
–Winston Churchill[1]

S torms will inevitably come upon us. Sometimes, we have advanced warnings. We watch the onset of symptoms like a storm chaser with a wary eye on a tropical disturbance. Other times, our caregiving duties appear out of nowhere like a tsunami wave: a sudden illness, a surgical complication, or an infection that derails recovery. These challenges can quickly spiral into a large storm. They can crash over us, overwhelm us, and devastate us. We are left with a picture of destruction and don't even know where or how to start the recovery effort. It can feel like our lives got turned upside down, and we may be so frightened and so overwhelmed that we feel like we can't take one more step forward.

LIE #8: I CAN'T TAKE ONE MORE STEP

Many days of caregiving felt unfair. I struggled with a lack of time, patience, and resources. I grumbled, not to the Lord, but to myself, about how He was treating me. Friend, have you been there, too? Despite knowing the absolute Truth that He loves you, have you ever felt unfavored or even abandoned? I would never have admitted it at the time, but the cold, hard truth was that I felt like God had turned against me and against my loved ones. I spent days wondering: what did I do to deserve this? Many mornings, I woke up feeling like I didn't have the strength to keep going, but other times seemed easier.

There were days when I got all the tasks completed and still had time to breathe. I reminisced with my loved ones about days gone by and watched the ghosts of memories bring a smile. I brought comfort with an embrace, a shared tear, or simply by holding a hand. I learned that even the "successful" days didn't run smoothly. Human emotional needs do not run like clockwork, and if you are too busy keeping the schedule, you might miss the moments when you can draw near to someone and bring Jesus with you.

Being truly present is part of doing the work; it's vital to engage in caregiving. We are called to care for more than just the physical body. Isaiah 40:8 tells us, "The grass withers and the flowers fall, but the word of our God endures forever." People are not so different from the grass and the flowers of the fields: our bodies will eventually wither and fade. It is difficult to watch loved ones age, and it is heartbreaking to watch them waste away due to sickness. We need to take care of the person's physical needs while also considering what God wants for them – both in body and in soul. The Gospel of Matthew is a good place to start as we seek answers to our questions about how to keep going when we feel depleted or discouraged in our calling:

> *"Then the King will say to those on his right, 'Come, you who are blessed by my Father; take your inheritance, the kingdom prepared for you since the creation of the world. For I was hungry and you gave me something to eat, I was thirsty and you gave me something to drink, I was a stranger and you invited me in, I needed clothes*

and you clothed me, I was sick and you looked after me,
I was in prison and you came to visit me.'"
— Matthew 25:34-36

Scripture tells us that we are indeed called to meet physical needs. Feed the hungry and give the thirsty something to drink – those are clear instructions – but Jesus shows us here that we are called to do more than that. "Visiting a prisoner" is about meeting an emotional/spiritual need, yet He includes it here with more tangible hands-on tasks. I believe we are to care for people while also honoring them. The angry and volatile Alzheimer's patient is a child of God. The stroke victim who can no longer communicate with you with her words is the daughter of the King. We may struggle in our situations, but we need to remember to look to Jesus as our ultimate example. He did not shy away from caring for the sick or the broken. Jesus tells us that what we do for them, we do for Him. He also tells us that the kingdom has already been prepared for us. We can rest in the safety of knowing our ultimate destination, even when the road of caregiving looks infinitely long and difficult. Remembering to lean on Jesus can help us to move forward, not by ourselves, but with Him at our sides.

Caregiving can be challenging, and our first and strongest support can be found in the Lord. He is the solid ground on which we stand, our refuge in the storms.

While each caregiving situation is unique, we can utilize various coping strategies. The Federal Emergency Management Agency (FEMA) uses one such strategy to direct its disaster response. Experts think of disasters as recurring events with four phases: Mitigation, Preparedness, Response, and Recovery.[2] Mitigation refers to plans that can minimize the impact of disasters. For example, a beach town might build a sea wall to help protect against hurricane damage. Preparedness would be boarding up windows and securing outdoor items before the arrival of a storm. Response is our reaction to the disaster in real-time, and recovery involves actions to return to a normal state.

Proactive planning can help alleviate some of the stress that occurs when health issues arise or recovery doesn't go according to plan. It would be impossible to list all the possible emergencies that could occur within a family, and I would not advise you to try to plan for each individual theoretical circumstance. However, many conditions do follow a predictable progression, and it is helpful to do what we can to make things as safe as possible for our loved ones by making minor adjustments to the physical environment that can help prevent accidents.

As people get older, they tend to have increasing difficulty with sight, balance, and mobility. Loose electrical cords or throw rugs are common hazards that can cause a fall. Another tactic for lowering the temperature during crisis situations is to channel your inner Boy Scout and be prepared! Keep a list (printed and electronic) of all current medications, allergies, and relevant medical and surgical history. Keep copies of identification and insurance information. Consider asking the doctor or pharmacist about getting an additional month's supply of prescriptions to have on hand. These seemingly minor tasks are, in fact, steps forward in your caregiving journey. These small activities remind me of the African proverb: "How do you eat an elephant? One bite at a time." When you find yourself believing the lie that you can't take one more step, look back at all the steps you have already walked. Rest in the knowledge that you didn't walk that road alone but rather with your loving Savior. We need to lean on Jesus as we walk, but we can get on our feet to walk with Him.

Mitigation and preparedness can help lessen the impact of a potential problem, or if we are lucky, they help avoid the problem in the first place. We are empowered to approach dynamic situations with a calm demeanor when we have the framework of an action plan to guide us. For instance, if your father-in-law is struggling to breathe, your response would likely begin with a phone call to 911. Once emergency responders are on scene, you or another loved one can quickly locate all the information his medical team will need to best take care of him. Your preparedness for emergency care will help to free you up to provide crucial emotional support.

Life is full of unexpected events that we can neither prevent nor control. We can, however, plan proactively to have ways to lessen the impact of medical setbacks. Let's imagine that you own a lovely house on the beach. Now, let's say that a hurricane has formed offshore and is predicted to make landfall directly over your home. It's unlikely that you would watch the weather reports and sit idly by, just hoping that the hurricane changes direction. Instead, you would board up the windows, buy bottled water, and make sure you have lots of batteries for the flashlights. Even so, the hurricane may still hit with a direct impact. Because we cannot control the storms, nor can we walk through them in our own strength, it is essential to rely on the strength of Jesus.

Let's look at this Scripture passage from the Gospel of Luke that tells a story about a storm, a plea, and an answer:

> "One day Jesus said to his disciples, 'Let us go over to the other side of the lake.' So they got into a boat and set out. As they sailed, he fell asleep. A squall came down on the lake, so that the boat was being swamped, and they were in great danger. The disciples went and woke him, saying, 'Master, Master, we're going to drown!' He got up and rebuked the wind and the raging waters; the storm subsided, and all was calm. 'Where is your faith?' he asked his disciples. In fear and amazement they asked one another, 'Who is this? He commands even the winds and the water, and they obey him.'"
>
> —Luke 8:22-25

Even the disciples cried out for help during the storm. In a moment of fear, they asked Jesus to save them from the fierce weather. Can you relate to their desperate plea? I have found myself feeling swamped from the proverbial waves many times. I wish I could say that as I cried out, Jesus showed up in bodily form and healed my broken situations, but He didn't. I kept crying out anyway, and I found that He would always offer shelter – He was always a safe harbor in the storm. More often than not, the storms continued to rage, but He gave me the strength to keep doing the work – day in and day out.

I understand the physical exhaustion and the emotional depletion that can happen when we are hard at work in the trenches of caregiving. I remember what it was like to wake up in the morning and feel so overwhelmed by the tasks in front of me that I struggled to even swing my feet over the side of the bed. For this reason, I want to encourage you that you can, in fact, get back up and start walking. Getting out of bed in the morning is a beginning. Feeding your dad breakfast is a small step. Every action you take is movement forward. It is hard and tiring, but we can do it with the help of Jesus. The truth is that none of us can journey in our own strength, but that doesn't mean that we can't take one more step. I was able to continue walking the road of caregiving, not in my own power, but in His, and the truth is friend – you can, too.

PERSPECTIVE SHIFT:

The demands and challenges we face as caregivers are ongoing, but we can reframe our experience by shifting our perspective. By learning to view our situation through the lens of God's Word and by leaning into the Truth it provides, we can begin to move from feeling fearful to hopeful, from embattled to empowered in Christ, and from unseen to unconditionally loved.

SACRIFICE: How much sleep are you getting on a nightly basis?

HOPE: Think about what "rest" means to you. Write some keywords in your journal.

INTERVENTION: Schedule a five-minute break during a busy day.

FOLLOW-UP: Write down what you did on your break.

TRUST: *Heavenly Father, we are weak, run-down, and feeling burdened. Wrap Your loving arms around us. Lead us by still waters and help us trust in the true rest that only You can give.*

Amen.

PART 5

EXPECT CHALLENGES

"'Though the mountains be shaken and the hills be removed, yet my unfailing love for you will not be shaken nor my covenant of peace be removed,' says the Lord, who has compassion on you."
– Isaiah 54:10

CHAPTER 9

OVERCOMING EXASPERATION

> *"Life is hard. Then you die. Then they throw dirt in your face.*
> *Then the worms eat you. Be grateful it happens in that order."*
> – David Gerrold[1]

*I*t was a gross rainy Tuesday morning, and we were running late for school. The traffic was crazy, and I was stuck at the stop sign, waiting to turn left. My son (the tender-hearted animal lover) looked out his window and asked alarmingly, "Is that cat DEAD?" *"Please, please, please don't let that be true,"* I thought as I looked out the window. You guessed it: the poor cat was sprawled on the side of the road, and my son had a clear view of the entire scene. The seconds ticked by as traffic refused to clear, and my son became increasingly distraught. I tried everything I knew to distract his attention away from the cat but to no avail. Friend, I hadn't even had my coffee yet, and I found myself contemplating how hard the rest of my day would be after this inauspicious start.

Finally, the traffic lifted, and I spent the rest of the ride to school trying to calm and comfort my son. As I suspected, my day did not get easier after that, and it is now referred to in my house as "Dead Cat Tuesday." As harsh as it may sound, my husband

and I use this phrase as a reminder that some days are just hard, and there's no sense in trying to convince ourselves otherwise. Many of us have moments when we tell ourselves the next lie, but we all face challenges, big and small, and sometimes we must wait for an opening in traffic, hit the gas, and move on.

LIE # 9: THIS SHOULDN'T BE SO HARD

We've all heard the expression: when it rains, it pours. That certainly felt true as my phone buzzed with an incoming call. I took a deep breath and braced myself. My father's number flashed across the screen, and I realized there must be a problem. He was at my house taking care of the children while I was at my mother-in-law's bedside in the intensive care unit (ICU). He wouldn't be calling me about something minor. *"This can't be good,"* I thought.

It had been a doozy of a week. We found my mother-in-law in the elevator of her home after she suffered an apparent stroke. We rushed her to the hospital and then navigated life-or-death decisions while we waited helplessly. Days later, just when we thought she had stabilized, seizures started. Then came the news that my father-in-law (in memory care) also began having seizures. "It's too much!" I cried silently to the Lord. "We are not strong enough for this."

I felt weighed down, mentally and physically exhausted, and I was running low on hope. It seemed like every step forward was quickly met with one or two steps back. I was trying to be an anchor of support for everyone. My husband sat in grim silence, and I prayed for the wisdom to know how to help him. I couldn't even imagine the impending loss he was facing. My children were showing signs of stress: extra arguing, nightmares, and crying. And now, *sigh*, my father was calling to tell me that my son was hurt. *"I can't even,"* I thought. *"It's not supposed to be this hard!"* In a season of extreme stress, I was unprepared to deal with another health crisis.

After receiving news a few days later from the orthopedist that my son had broken his foot, I felt like I, too, was broken. Individually, his broken foot was not earth-shattering, but when piled on top of hospitalizations, pre-existing worry, and grief, it was enough to send me spiraling. My feelings about the situation were out of proportion to the diagnosis of a fractured foot. In the grand scheme of life, his injury was not a big deal, but when added to everything else that was going on at the time, it was overwhelming. At the time, I was laser-focused on trying to manage (control) the situation, and I didn't stop to turn my eyes to the Lord. Relying on my own strength, I quickly discovered that I could no longer shoulder the load I was faced with.

My son did not have a waterproof cast, and one evening, he accidentally managed to let his foot slide off the edge of the tub and into the bath water. A wet cast meant that I had to take him back to the doctor for a new one. This was the moment that sent me over the edge. I helped him dry everything as best we could, and then I retreated to my room and cried. This was not a few silent tears running down my cheeks kind of episode, but rather, ugly gut-wrenching sobs shaking my entire body. I struggled for big gulps of air as the emotions that had piled up finally broke free. As my tears eventually subsided, I found myself wondering, *"Why can't we catch a break?"*

Why do we expect things to be easy? We want to take the easy way out, make it to Easy Street, or use the Staples® Easy Button. If only those were real options! Following Jesus does not guarantee us a life without difficulty. Scripture gives us many stories of this truth. The book of Ruth is a story full of hardship, loss, and redemption, and it's a beautiful example of God being with us even as we walk through hard times. Naomi left Bethlehem under difficult circumstances. There was famine, and Naomi and her family were facing starvation:

> *"In the days when the judges ruled, there was a famine in the land. So a man from Bethlehem in Judah, together with his wife and two sons, went to live for a while in the country of Moab. The man's name was Elimelek, his wife's name was Naomi, and the names of his two sons were Mahlon and Kilion. They were Ephrathites from Bethlehem, Judah. And they went to Moab and lived there."*
>
> — Ruth 1:1-2

The distance from Bethlehem to Moab was approximately 50 miles.[2] It was not an easy journey on foot, but at least Naomi had her husband and sons as protectors. Scripture doesn't give us a lot of detail about their years in Moab, but we know that the sons both married Moabite women, Ruth and Orpah. They lived there for about 10 years, and during that time, Naomi suffered the loss not only of her husband but, subsequently, both of her sons. Losing a spouse is hard but often part of the natural order of things. Losing a child must come with heartbreak that takes your very breath away, and Naomi lost two. I can only imagine the despair she must have felt and how hard everything must have seemed for her. There was nothing left for her in Moab, and when she heard that the famine in Judah was over, she decided to return home.

> *"When Naomi heard in Moab that the Lord had come to the aid of his people by providing food for them, she and her daughters-in-law prepared to return home from there. With her two daughters-in-law she left the place where she had been living and set out on the road that would take them back to the land of Judah."*
>
> — Ruth 1:6-7

I suspect Naomi thought her journey from Bethlehem to Moab was challenging. My family can't even manage a long day in the comfort of an air-conditioned vehicle without getting grouchy. Naomi's family had no such comforts; rather, they faced a physically hard journey with an uncertain ending. Naomi's family fled to Moab in a bid to survive, and ten years later, Naomi likely believed that returning to Bethlehem would give her the best chance of survival. Fear is a powerful motivator, and, we too, are at risk of making unwise decisions when we act out of fear instead of faith.

Unlike Naomi, we have the privilege of knowing the entire story. With time and distance, we can see how the Lord provided for Naomi despite outward appearances. It's true that Naomi was widowed and then lost her two sons. Her heartbreak was real, but God stayed with her through the hard times. He was with her when she left Bethlehem, and He was with her when she finally returned home. Naomi's eyes were on the challenges, not on the provisions. While her emotions led her to the conclusion that the Lord had turned away from her, He was, in fact, continuing to provide, to make a way, to set her on a journey towards home and towards redemption. Here we see Naomi's short-sighted response to her circumstances:

> *"So the two women went on until they came to Bethlehem. When they arrived in Bethlehem, the whole town was stirred because of them, and the women exclaimed, 'Can this be Naomi?' 'Don't call me Naomi,' she told them. 'Call me Mara, because the Almighty has made my life very bitter. I went away full, but the Lord has brought me back empty. Why call me Naomi? The Lord has afflicted me; the Almighty has brought misfortune upon me.'"*
>
> —Ruth 1:19-21

Have you ever felt as if God Himself has turned against you? I know I have, and it has come up again and again through different valleys in my life. I find that it is much easier to accept life as His will when things are easy. Sometimes, though, the misfortunes keep piling up; one crisis follows the next, and before we know it, we feel bitter like Naomi. We hold onto our hurts and our disappointments and wish things were easier, but the truth is that we will all face hardship. Who among us hasn't grieved or faced loss? Who hasn't sat at a bedside or stood at a graveside and yearned for relief? Even Jesus experienced grief. The gospel of John gives us a beautiful account of Jesus sharing emotions of grief when He arrives on scene after his friend Lazarus had died three days prior:

> "When Mary reached the place where Jesus was and saw him, she fell at his feet and said, 'Lord, if you had been here, my brother would not have died.' When Jesus saw her weeping, and the Jews who had come along with her also weeping, he was deeply moved in spirit and troubled. 'Where have you laid him?' he asked. 'Come and see, Lord,' they replied. Jesus wept."
>
> –John 11:32–35

He wept. Jesus' grief was raw and real, but friend, this is good news! We have a God who feels our pain, who understands every part of our humanity. Jesus walked His own hard roads, and He walks our hard roads with us. He walks with us, supports us, and provides for us.

> "So Naomi returned from Moab accompanied by Ruth the Moabite, her daughter-in-law, arriving in Bethlehem as the barley harvest was beginning."
>
> – Ruth 1:22

Naomi and Ruth arrived as the barley harvest was beginning. Why is this detail important? They arrived at the beginning of the harvest because God's timing is perfect. Naomi fled from famine and returned to harvest. His provision was not dependent on Naomi's attitude. He was still there with her, guiding her steps as she proclaimed to the entire town that He had turned against her. God's provision for us, likewise, is not dependent on our actions or abilities. His grace is a gift freely given. We need only to open our eyes and our hearts to see it.

> *"I have told you these things, so that in me you may have peace. In this world you will have trouble. But take heart! I have overcome the world."*
>
> – John 16:33

Believers are not promised easy lives free from trouble and heartache. Quite the opposite, in fact, is true. We *will* have trouble. We live in a broken world with broken people. We face disease, disability, and death. We worry and we mourn. We pray and we cry out and we do our very best to take care of our loved ones, and friend, we cannot do this by ourselves. God knows this truth and He has provided a way for us.

> *"For God so loved the world that he gave his one and only Son, that whoever believes in him shall not perish but have eternal life. For God did not send his Son into the world to condemn the world, but to save the world through him."*
>
> – John 3:16-17

We live in the now and the not yet. We have the saving grace of Jesus, but we still wait for Him to return. Meanwhile, we spend our days in a fallen, sinful, broken world that comes with all kinds of pain and heartache. We will suffer, mourn, and struggle – all of which Jesus understands because He has been there, my friend. Jesus shares our humanity and invites us to trust in Him and to know that He will not leave us.

Consider adding some visual cues to your environment to remind you of God's love and faithfulness. It doesn't have to be fancy or expensive, just serve as a reminder of the Truth. For instance, I have a practice I call "sticky note Scripture." When my children were struggling with something, I would find relevant and encouraging Scripture, which I would write on a sticky note. I placed the notes on headboards to cover them while they slept, on mirrors so they would see God's Word first thing in the morning, and in backpacks or lunch boxes to serve as an anchor point during their day. When you feel exasperated and resentful, remember that God will never leave you – even during hard times. The truth is that He is there waiting to help you, to walk with you, and to help you overcome the difficulties of this world.

PERSPECTIVE SHIFT:

The demands and challenges we face as caregivers are ongoing, but we can reframe our experience by shifting our perspective. By learning to view our situation through the lens of God's Word and by leaning into the Truth it provides, we can begin to move from feeling fearful to hopeful, from embattled to empowered in Christ, and from unseen to unconditionally loved.

SACRIFICE: What are the two hardest things in your caregiving journey?

HOPE: Check out the following Scripture verses for some encouragement:

Isaiah 41:10; Philippians 4:13; and 1 Corinthians 15:58

INTERVENTION: Start a journal, or use the notes app on your phone to keep track of solutions/tricks that have made caregiving easier for you. Additionally, find a convenient system for tracking medications, appointments, etc.

FOLLOW-UP: Assess how your current organizational system is functioning and make any changes as needed.

TRUST: *Heavenly Father, You cared for us so much that You gave us the life of Your beloved Son. That gift is indeed our salvation, and we look to You with hope and trust as we walk through hard times.*

Amen.

CHAPTER 10

GRACE IN ANGUISH

I felt like the day was never going to end. My anxiety and worry had been playing havoc with my sleep schedule, and my patience was running thin. My son had a stomach virus, and I was keeping tabs on older relatives, but by and large, it was a typical day. Irritation got the best of me, and I snapped at one of the kids. Realizing my mistake, I stepped out of the room and took a moment to collect myself and pray. I reminded myself that this was the day the Lord had made, and I should be glad in it.

I returned to my routine with renewed energy and a sense of peace. Just then, my son yelled, "Mom! I need help!" I rushed into his room to discover that he was vomiting. All over his bed. And just like that, the negative thoughts took command as I announced, "This day can suck it!"

LIE #10: I SHOULDN'T BE SO MAD

I was mad. One day, life was normal, and the next — bam — I felt like I'd been run over. It seemed like nothing was fair, and frankly, I was over it. I didn't want to spend another late night in the ER or "sleep" on the hospital pull-out couch, or go to the pharmacy for the 48th time. I was tired of vending machine food and the smell of hospital soap. And if I had to listen to another ten minutes of an IV machine beeping, I was going to lose my mind. I had a headache, my face was swollen, and my eyes were stinging from the tears I shed as I washed my hair in the teeny tiny hospital shower that morning. I didn't want to be here, not in this crisis, building, or frame of mind.

So, now what? What should I do when it seems like I can't get it right? How am I supposed to "rejoice and be glad" when I have a ring-side seat to immense suffering? And how am I supposed to respond when the suffering becomes mine? Honestly, I had no idea.

I didn't know what to do, but I was pretty sure I wasn't supposed to feel so enraged. I was mad at my circumstances, at myself, and... at God. Is that even allowed? What happens if we are angry with the Lord?

It feels wrong to admit I was mad at the Almighty. I was angry with God and simultaneously ashamed of my anger, which, in turn, made it harder for me to be honest about my feelings. I was convinced that my aggrieved feelings were an affront to God, and yet I couldn't help but wonder, *"What did I do to deserve this? Why would You let this happen? And furthermore, if You're so loving and merciful, what's up with all this suffering?"*

I had questions, but I held them tightly in the secret places of my heart. There was no way I was going to ask those things out loud. What would people say? Or worse, what would they not say but think about me anyway? I already felt so alone, and the last thing I needed was for everyone to discover my ugly black heart and decide they didn't want to be around me anymore.

Suffering is hard to understand, especially when it is personal. It's one thing to see images of far-away wars on the evening news and shake our heads at the sadness of pain and suffering. It's another thing altogether when the suffering is up close and personal. We move from watching suffering to witnessing it.

Susan's Story:

Susan's mom, Joy, suffered from lung disease, which often caused breathing difficulties. Joy was afflicted with the physical symptoms of her illness and had terrible coughing fits where she struggled to get air. She was drowning in her own phlegm. Joy, in fact, was tormented to the point that she would cry out to God, "Lord, please take me! Please take me!" Susan could overhear everything from her bedroom. She heard the coughing and gasping for air. She heard her mom begging God to let her die. Joy was not suffering alone – Susan was suffering with her. As difficult as it is to lose a loved one, Susan would cry and, through her tears, ask the Lord to take her mother home to heaven.

Susan was not just watching her mother suffer during those last weeks; she was witnessing it. She stood by, feeling helpless but offering any support she could as her dear mother battled to draw breath. The anguish was immense for them both. Much as mothers are distressed when their children struggle, the flip side is also true. Children (even as grown adults) are pained when they witness a parent suffering. Their connection is almost visceral. To witness suffering is to be a part of it, and oftentimes, we respond with feelings of anger or even rage.

Have you ever felt angry in your suffering or perhaps even felt as though you have been abandoned? I sure have. The Bible gives us examples, not only of suffering but of how God's people responded to it. We've already seen how Naomi responded to her many losses as she told others that the Lord had made her bitter, but hers is not the only story we can look to for wisdom.

The Old Testament gives us the story of Jeremiah, the weeping prophet. In those days, Judah had turned away from the Lord. The people were worshiping idols and even practicing atrocities such as child sacrifice. God sent Jeremiah to warn them to repent. The people, though, were prideful, and they believed that God would not bring destruction on them because they were His chosen people. Instead of heeding Jeremiah's words, they followed false prophets who proclaimed good tidings and prosperity – in other words, they only listened to people who told them what they wanted to hear.

> *"This is the word that came to Jeremiah from the Lord: 'Stand at the gate of the Lord's house and there proclaim this message: 'Hear the word of the Lord, all you people of Judah who come through these gates to worship the Lord. This is what the Lord Almighty, the God of Israel, says: Reform your ways and your actions, and I will let you live in this place.'"*
>
> – Jeremiah 7:1-3

> *"If you really change your ways and your actions and deal with each other justly, if you do not oppress the foreigner, the fatherless or the widow and do not shed innocent blood in this place, and if you do not follow other gods to your own harm, then I will let you live in this place, in the land I gave your ancestors for ever and ever."*
>
> – Jeremiah 7:5-6

Like many of us, the people of that time were stubborn and continued doing what was right in their own eyes. They didn't want to hear messages about impending doom and destruction. Jeremiah wasn't telling the people what they wanted to hear, and he wasn't winning any popularity contests. They didn't want to hear his warning or change their behavior, and their recalcitrance started to wear on Jeremiah.

Can you identify with Jeremiah's frustration? I know I've been in the situation where I'm taking care of someone, and I see the slow-moving train wreck approaching. I try every way I can think of to get my point across and avoid the oncoming problem, but people won't listen. What comes next? Usually, I get frustrated, and that frustration turns into anger. Anger at my situation will oftentimes harden my heart, and before I know it, I'm feeling angry, not only with the person who didn't listen but also with God. Let's take a look at some Scripture that shows us some of Jeremiah's heart:

> *"You deceived me, Lord, and I was deceived, you overpowered me and prevailed. I am ridiculed all day long; everyone mocks me. Whenever I speak, I cry out proclaiming violence and destruction. So the work of the Lord has brought me insult and reproach all day long."*
>
> – Jeremiah 20:7-8

Here, Jeremiah takes his feelings to the Lord, just as we are supposed to do. Jeremiah, one of God's chosen prophets, complained to the Lord!

Caring for people is hard. It's hard when you are focused on one individual's health needs, and it's hard when you are shepherding the spiritual lives of an entire people. Overwhelm, anger, frustration, and discouragement on our parts will not surprise the Lord, nor will it deter Him from walking with us while we grumble. Like Jeremiah, we are called to be obedient even in the midst of opposition and challenges.

Looking back, I can see that unresolved pain led me to build walls around my heart instead of building my relationship with Jesus, and in doing so, I only prolonged my own suffering. I eventually learned that I'm better off taking my feelings to the Lord rather than trying to stuff them down and pretend everything is fine. "Fine" is a go-to word for caregivers. We use it out of habit, because we don't have time to explain a complicated situation, or because we don't want to admit our true feelings. Instead of burying our anger, we need to learn to take it to the Lord. It's okay to tell God that you are furious, fatigued, or frightened. The truth is that He already knows how you feel, and He won't turn away from you – not even when you're angry, bitter, or doubtful. When you are honest with God about your feelings, you will find comfort in His steady presence. You will build a closer relationship by offering Him your vulnerable heart, and He will, in turn, continue to draw you ever closer to Himself.

As caregivers, we often give intimate care to another person, and this can bring special challenges. Changing adult diapers isn't fun. Cleaning an infected wound can turn the stomach with the smell of bacteria. Answering the same question for the 30th time in a day can frustrate even the most patient of us. When you go to the Lord, try taking your filter off. Give Him the raw, real, heart-wrenching truth of your day, and ask Him to help you manage your normal human emotions. Friend, when you feel defeated, when you are struggling with the challenges of your journey when your heart is broken into a million little pieces, remember that Jesus is the one who can help you put the pieces back together.

We all get angry sometimes. Walking through hard times and hard emotions is just part of our human experience, but the good news is that Jesus helps us navigate the exhausting uphill roads. He gives us His grace, and the Bible tells us:

> *"But he said to me, 'My grace is sufficient for you, for my power is made perfect in weakness.' Therefore I will boast all the more gladly about my weaknesses, so that Christ's power may rest on me."*
>
> – **2 Corinthians 12:9**

His grace is sufficient. Your humanity is a gift from God Himself, and so important that He sent His Son Jesus to us – fully man and fully God – to save us from our sin, all while understanding our human hearts.

Have you ever had a problem and felt like you needed to talk to someone who had been through the same situation? A woman facing an unwanted divorce probably won't seek out a happily married friend to help process her heartbreak. We reach out to people who we think will understand us and support us. There is a bond that comes from shared experience. Our Heavenly Father gave us a perfect model in His Son Jesus. He lived an earthly life and experienced His own joys and disappointments. He has been hungry and tired. He has faced rejection. He understands our emotions because He walked among us. When you are in anguish, when your heart cries out for relief, you can call on the powerful name of Jesus who, by His grace, will help you through it – and that, my friend, is the truth.

PERSPECTIVE SHIFT:

The demands and challenges we face as caregivers are ongoing, but we can reframe our experience by shifting our perspective. By learning to view our situation through the lens of God's Word and by leaning into the Truth it provides, we can begin to move from feeling fearful to hopeful, from embattled to empowered in Christ, and from unseen to unconditionally loved.

SACRIFICE: Write down three things that you have felt angry about in the last week.

HOPE: Give yourself permission to be angry without feeling guilty, but think about what you want for the days ahead.

INTERVENTION: Take your hard feelings to the Lord and ask Him to soften your heart.

FOLLOW-UP: Find a time during each day to check in with yourself and address any anger issues with prayer.

TRUST: *Lord, it is scary to bring our negative emotions before You. Draw us near, we pray. Help us to be completely honest with You, to trust in You always, and to surrender our hearts to Your will.*

Amen.

PART 6:

MEET PEOPLE WHERE THEY ARE, WITH MERCY

"Therefore, as God's chosen people, holy and dearly loved, clothe yourselves with compassion, kindness, humility, gentleness and patience."
– Colossians 3:12

CHAPTER 11

BEYOND RECOGNITION

"Most people return small favors, acknowledge middling ones and repay greater ones – with ingratitude."
– Benjamin Franklin[1]

I was driving down the highway going – ahem – somewhat above the speed limit. As I cruised with left-lane traffic, I noticed a car approaching behind me at a higher rate of speed. I signaled to get into the right lane but was unable to do so as the driver behind me gunned it and came very close to the back of my car as he darted into the right lane, zoomed past me, and then quickly cut back in front of me. My heart raced as I realized how close he came to clipping my car and sending us both spinning out of control. And then I saw it – a beautiful sight that made my heart sing with joy – the flashing blue lights of a police car.

How great is the desire to see people get what they deserve? Friend, I must admit, sometimes the feeling overtakes me. I laughed out loud as I drove past the other driver, who was now pulled over on the shoulder of the highway, presumably getting a ticket. I was experiencing what the Germans refer to as *schadenfreude*, which is defined as "the emotional experience of pleasure in response to another's misfortune."[2] As I reflect on this situation now, I wonder what his circumstances were that day. Would I have been so quick to delight in his experience if I knew the whole story? Maybe that driver was rushing an injured child to the hospital or responding to an urgent call from home. Perhaps he was running late and one more mark against him could result in getting fired. I had no way of knowing why he sped past me that day, but I reacted out of my own experience, out of how I was feeling that day, without taking his circumstances into consideration. In other words, I was without mercy.

I don't know about you, but I'm not at my best when I'm in pain, scared, or stressed. Aren't these the times when we are most in need of mercy? I'm sure there have been times when I was in need of care but not appreciative of the person taking care of me. I had to have my gallbladder removed when I was four weeks postpartum from the birth of my oldest child. I was terrified as the anesthesiologist talked me through things, and I don't remember much after that, but I've heard stories. These days, I actually apologize to my nurses in advance – I've been told I can be combative and demanding when coming out of anesthesia. Medical professionals deal with difficult patients on a regular basis, but doing so as a family caregiver can be more challenging. You have an established relationship with your loved one, and their unkind behavior can lead to strong emotional reactions on your part. It can be tempting to wash your hands of caregiving responsibilities and give them what they deserve. God doesn't give us what we deserve; rather, He extends His grace and mercy and we should seek to follow His model.

I want to point out that being merciful to someone is not the same thing as tolerating an abusive situation. If you are dealing with abuse, there is help. Please see the resource list at the back of the book.

As caregivers, it can be hard to keep our compassion at the forefront when the person we take care of is lashing out. Sometimes, our situations are so challenging that we are tempted to walk away as we buy into the misconception that we can't keep going if people aren't grateful.

LIE #11: I CAN'T KEEP CAREGIVING IF I'M UNAPPRECIATED

There are many tasks in life that feel like thankless jobs — laundry and dishes come quickly to mind. By and large, we go through life taking care of business without needing constant thanks and recognition. I've discovered, though, that over time, a lack of acknowledgment or, worse, a sense of entitlement from others can wear us down. It's one thing to feel unappreciated, but it's a whole other ballgame when the person we take care of is in active opposition to us or even angry with us.

You might ask yourself, *"Why is Mom being so difficult?"* or think, *"I wish Dad wouldn't be so resistant to help."* I want to reassure you that these situations are common, and it can help to put yourself in the place of the person you take care of. Perhaps Mom is acting out because she is in pain that she hasn't told you about. Dad might be pushing people away because he doesn't want them to discover his issues with memory loss. There are many reasons why the person we take care of might not react to us in a positive way.

Maria's Story:

Jennifer raised her voice and took a swing at her stepdaughter. Maria was just trying to take care of her stepmom, but dementia had rendered Jennifer incapable of understanding the situation. "I don't need your help!" she shouted. The disease often caused her to act out in anger and frustration. Sometimes, there were warning signs and opportunities to de-escalate the situation, but other times, Jennifer's angry outbursts were unpredictable. When Maria sensed Jennifer's anger building, she would calmly tell her, "Look in my eyes. I'm doing this because I'm trying to help you — because I love you."

Maria knew that Jennifer's behavior towards her wasn't personal, but it still stung. The woman she'd loved for all these years had seemingly turned against her, rejecting not only her help but, oftentimes, even her physical presence. Jennifer's rejection didn't stop Maria from taking care of her, but it sure did make the job harder. In fact, Maria often had to physically protect herself from Jennifer by crossing her arms and blocking her face as Jennifer tried to hit her. Maria understood the reality of the situation — if Jennifer injured her, then she wouldn't be able to provide the care that was needed. For Jennifer's part, as is often the case with dementia-related diseases, she lacked insight into the situation and wouldn't remember the unpleasant interactions. Maria soldiered on without a shred of remorse from her stepmom. She understood that she would never receive appreciation from Jennifer, and while that was difficult, she took care of her until her final day.

Stories like Maria's break my heart, but they are more common than most people realize. Any disease or injury that affects the brain can result in memory issues or changes in personality and behavior. In Jennifer's case, disease was driving her behavior, but sometimes, caregivers find themselves faced with other behavioral challenges from the people they take care of. Some of us are navigating situations in which we have always had a fraught relationship with our care recipient. People who have a history of being unkind or ill-tempered are unlikely to develop a sunny disposition because they need someone to take care of them. In fact, they are more likely to respond to their changed reality with anger and frustration. People who suffer from mental health disorders or substance abuse issues still have those diagnoses after they suffer a stroke or a heart attack. If they were difficult to deal with before, chances are they will continue to be so. It's not uncommon to have an adversarial relationship with your care recipient, and this can lead to feelings of impatience and discontent.

I can't help but wonder — did Naomi ever tell Ruth, "Thank you"? Scripture doesn't mention it. Ruth took care of Naomi anyway. Jesus calls us to care for others, not as they deserve, but as He would care for them.

Have you ever found yourself feeling disappointed when your contributions are overlooked? Or perhaps you've even been in the position where you start to question if others value you as a person. It's hard to keep putting other people first when you are so often pushed to last place. The gospel of Mark presents a story where Jesus too, knew what it felt like to be unappreciated:

> *"They went to a place called Gethsemane, and Jesus said to his disciples, 'Sit here while I pray.' He took Peter, James and John along with him, and he began to be deeply distressed and troubled. 'My soul is overwhelmed with sorrow to the point of death,' he said to them. 'Stay here and keep watch.' Going a little farther, he fell to the ground and prayed that if possible the hour might pass from him. 'Abba, Father,' he said, 'everything is possible for you. Take this cup from me. Yet not what I will, but what you will.' Then he returned to his disciples and found them sleeping. 'Simon,' he said to Peter, 'are you asleep? Couldn't you keep watch for one hour? Watch and pray so that you will not fall into temptation. The spirit is willing but the flesh is weak.' Once more he went away and prayed the same thing. When he came back, he again found them sleeping, because their eyes were heavy. They did not know what to say to him. Returning the third time, he said to them, 'Are you still sleeping and resting? Enough! The hour has come. Look, the Son of Man is delivered into the hands of sinners. Rise! Let us go! Here comes my betrayer!'"*

> – Mark 14:32-42

Jesus wasn't asking much of the disciples in this situation. His request was a simple one: keep watch and pray – and yet, they don't. They don't keep watch, and they don't pray; they fall asleep! Jesus knows that He is about to be taken into custody, knows what He is going to do to save us, and He certainly knows the pain that awaits Him. Jesus says that He is "overwhelmed with sorrow to the point of death." Jesus, the one who has been their teacher, their confidant, and their friend, is about to become their Savior, and they couldn't stay awake and pray. How disappointing.

The disciples let Jesus down, but while I imagine He felt hurt, He didn't turn His back on them. Jesus loved the disciples, and He understood their human frailties. They fell asleep, but Jesus went to them, woke them, and called them to come with Him. Jesus walked willingly into the hands of His accusers, and He walked willingly to the cross. He laid down his very life to save me, to save you, and to save the disciples who couldn't stay awake. Jesus' mercy meets us where we are.

We take care of others because it is the right thing to do. Jesus doesn't tell us to take care of people when it's convenient or when we will be celebrated for doing so. But rather we know this truth:

> *"The King will reply, 'Truly I tell you, whatever you did for one of the least of these brothers and sisters of mine, you did for me.'"*
>
> –Matthew 25:40

We learned earlier in this book that caregivers are kingdom workers. As such, we do not work for others but for the Lord. It's nice to receive recognition or appreciation from others, and it's not unreasonable for us to desire to be encouraged in that way. While it is normal to long for validation of our efforts, we may not get it from the people around us or even from the very person we are caring for. In fact, sometimes, our care recipients are in such a bad emotional state that they will lash out at us in anger and frustration. It helps to remember that they, too, are children of God, and you are serving them as you act as the very hands and feet of Jesus. If you find yourself feeling unseen and unappreciated, try journaling or talking to God by stating what you have done for your loved one. Now, remembering that what you do for the least of these, you do for Jesus, evaluate what you did during the day. My friend, know this: your work is sacred and sacrificial and SEEN by your Heavenly Father. Your caregiving has eternal consequences, and with every interaction, you have the honor of bringing Jesus with you. Truly, we can keep walking through the storm – not for praise and appreciation – but for Jesus.

PERSPECTIVE SHIFT:

The demands and challenges we face as caregivers are ongoing, but we can reframe our experience by shifting our perspective. By learning to view our situation through the lens of God's Word and by leaning into the Truth it provides, we can begin to move from feeling fearful to hopeful, from embattled to empowered in Christ, and from unseen to unconditionally loved.

SACRIFICE: Write down the last incident that made you feel unappreciated.

HOPE: Now, write down how you think God views that situation.

INTERVENTION: What do you think is the best part about being a caregiver? Write one or two positive aspects of your journey.

FOLLOW-UP: Has a shift in your thinking helped you to reset when you feel like you can't keep going?

TRUST: *Most merciful God, our hearts hurt when we feel unseen, unloved, or unappreciated. Come close to us, Lord, whisper Your Truths in our ears. Remind us that our strength does not come from other people* *but solely from You. Be with us as we continue to pour out care for Your precious children that You entrusted into our hands.*

Amen.

CHAPTER 12

BREAKING FREE FROM THE FEAR OF FALLING SHORT

"I have not failed. I've just found 10,000 ways that
won't work."
– Thomas A. Edison[1]

I freaked out when I realized what I had done. Our dog gets two pills every day – a vitamin C and an allergy medication – that we store in a kitchen cabinet with lots of other medicine. A sense of hesitation crept over me right after he wolfed down the cheese pocket that I made for his pills. Something felt off, and when I looked at the bottles on the kitchen counter, it hit me – one of them was wrong! I had accidentally given my dog acetaminophen instead of loratadine! A quick Google search informed me that I had made a serious mistake, indeed, as acetaminophen can be toxic for dogs. The pill bottles in question were the same color, and the pills themselves were the same shape, but the outcome was the same: I might have just poisoned my dog.

We all make mistakes: big ones, small ones, important ones, and insignificant ones. Thankfully, my dog was fine, but I certainly fell short that day. Who among us hasn't experienced that knot in our stomachs, that feeling of dread when we realize we messed up? When I make a mistake, my first reaction is often to beat myself up about it. I have somehow bought into believing that my best isn't good enough, and even worse – I feel undeserving of mercy.

LIE # 12: MY BEST ISN'T GOOD ENOUGH

I don't know anyone who appreciates being micromanaged, especially by people who don't know what they're talking about. Friend, have you been in the situation where someone who has very little knowledge of the day-to-day responsibilities of being a caregiver swoops in and thinks they know better than you? I have, and I've got to tell you – I found it rather irritating. I don't appreciate the dismissal of my efforts, my knowledge, and my sacrifice – especially from someone who doesn't have the lay of the land. I grew resentful because it felt like no matter what I did, it wasn't good enough to please people.

I'm going to share an unfortunate truth with you: sometimes, we won't have everything we need in our roles as caregivers, and this can make us feel like we aren't doing a good job. Some of us are blessed with financial resources, while others pinch pennies to pay for the necessary medical care. Some of us have a great support network made up of family members and friends, while others are isolated and feeling lonely. Caregivers who live in large metro areas likely have better access to specialists and home care professionals than those who live in more rural settings. No two situations are the same, but we do have something in common: we all face challenges. They might be financial, familial, emotional, or spiritual, but any way you slice it, caregiving is hard.

Barbara's Story:

Barbara is a retired nurse educator who looked after her 90-year-old mother, Rose. Falls are a risk for many elderly people, and Rose was no exception. She fell at the nursing home, and staff later discovered her on the floor in a pool of blood. Rose was rushed to the hospital and diagnosed with a brain bleed. Barbara was a fantastic advocate for her mom and met with Rose's care providers daily. As Rose improved, she was allowed to eat, and this was when Barbara belatedly realized something important: Rose didn't have her dentures. Rose wasn't eating normally because she was missing her teeth! "Where are her teeth?" Barbara urgently asked the nurse. The nurse didn't know where Rose's dentures were. Barbara sprang into action and searched the hospital room high and low, but she didn't find the teeth.

By this point, Barbara was feeling rather nervous. The COVID-19 pandemic had shut everything down, including many dental offices. Barbara, a retired nurse with financial resources and plenty of family support, found herself lacking what she most needed: a set of teeth. Armed with more knowledge than the average caregiver, Barbara tracked down the staff member that was with Rose at the time of the accident, knowing that she would have overseen the process of transferring Rose onto the ambulance. The staff member had wisely taken some of Rose's belongings for safekeeping – including the dentures. Hallelujah! Rose hadn't been eating properly without her dentures. She had been embarrassed about not having her teeth and withdrew socially. By locating and returning Rose's dentures, Barbara was able to put her mom on a straightforward path to recovery. As you can see, sometimes it really is the little things that matter.

We can see here that this situation was not Barbara's doing, but she still experienced feelings of guilt. *"Why didn't I catch this mistake sooner?"* she asked herself. She was so focused on the problem at hand that she lost sight of all the ways in which she was an amazing caregiver. Accidents happen, and things get lost sometimes, and it isn't in our best interest to hold onto the inevitable missteps, even if it was our fault. Sometimes, we make mistakes and need to engage in corrective action, but sometimes we just need to file it away as a lesson learned. Instead, we often hold on to every little detail of what we did wrong – as if that would somehow fix anything. We might feel embarrassed, guilty, and ashamed that we made a mistake – that our best wasn't good enough. We mistakenly buy into the belief that those emotions should be allowed to keep their grip on our hearts.

Guilt and shame are bullies. They follow us around, whispering insults that they somehow know will pierce the vulnerable places of our hearts. And like scared little kids, we try to run away. We distance ourselves from the hurtful words, and we try not to think about our failures, of all the times we just didn't measure up. We collect our mistakes like baseball cards and hide them away in the recesses of our hearts. I tell you this because I've collected a lot of mistakes over the years, and I understand the heartache that comes from believing the lie that my best isn't good enough.

Training took over as I approached my father-in-law with the pain medication from hospice. He was in his final days of his battle with Alzheimer's Disease and very much the picture of human suffering — bedridden, skeletal, and mostly nonverbal. This man was, in his prime, a brilliant and well-respected physician. He, who had given so much of his life providing medical care for others, was now dependent on us to take care of him. And I failed.

As a nurse, I had been trained to do certain things when administering medication: confirm the patient name and date of birth, check for allergies, double-check the medication and the dosage, and communicate clearly with my patient. When my father-in-law needed morphine, I didn't deviate from this procedure, and my by-the-book medication administration sent him into a panic. I announced, "I have morphine for you, Doyle.

It will help with your pain." This was a mistake that haunted me for years. In his career as a physician, he witnessed first-hand the ravages that came from opioid abuse. He was extremely careful about his own use of medications, but I failed to account for this as I approached him with the syringe in my hand. He needed morphine. The family and the hospice care providers were all in agreement that he should not spend his last hours on this earth in agonizing pain.

He deserved so much better than this – he deserved better than this disease, he deserved better than being trapped in his own body, and he deserved better than to feel afraid. He was suffering, and I made it worse. I approached him, stroked his forehead, and talked softly to him. I explained that we could tell that he was hurting and that we were going to help him. And then I told him that I had morphine.

His reaction was strong and immediate. To him, "morphine" was a bad word, the enemy, that wolf in sheep's clothing, and he wanted no part of it. I can still see the look of fear in his eyes. The very last thing I wanted to do at that moment was cause him any more pain, and yet, that's exactly what I had done. Oh, friend, the shame I felt was strong and long-lasting, and I somehow believed in those moments that I deserved to hold on to those guilty feelings.

Guilt and shame are powerful bullies, but Jesus is a Savior and Redeemer. Throughout His ministry, He interacted with those who society deemed unacceptable — tax collectors, lepers, and prostitutes – to name a few. Once, when Jesus was traveling through Samaria on His way to Galilee, He stopped in a town called Sychar. Jesus, hot from the noonday sun and tired from His travels, sat down near a well.

> "When a Samaritan woman came to draw water, Jesus said to her, 'Will you give me a drink?' The Samaritan woman said to him, 'You are a Jew and I am a Samaritan woman. How can you ask me for a drink?'"
>
> – John 4:7-9

Right off the bat, Jesus is speaking with a woman who would traditionally have been shunned by Jews. Additionally, the woman was by herself, not with another group of women as was the custom. Most of the women in town would have come to the well together in the morning to draw water before the heat of the day was upon them. The Samaritan woman was not welcome with the other women, but Jesus does not hesitate to engage with her.

> *"Jesus answered her, 'If you knew the gift of God and who it is that asks you for a drink, you would have asked him and he would have given you living water.' 'Sir,' the woman said, 'you have nothing to draw with and the well is deep. Where can you get this living water? Are you greater than our father Jacob, who gave us the well and drank from it himself, as did also his sons and his livestock?' Jesus answered, 'Everyone who drinks this water will be thirsty again, but whoever drinks the water I give them will never thirst. Indeed, the water I give them will become in them a spring of water welling up to eternal life.' The woman said to him, 'Sir, give me this water so that I won't get thirsty and have to keep coming here to draw water.' He told her, 'Go, call your husband and come back.' 'I have no husband,' she replied. Jesus said to her, 'You are right when you say you have no husband. The fact is, you have had five husbands, and the man you now have is not your husband. What you have just said is quite true.'"*
> — John 4:10-18

Jesus goes on to tell the woman, this sinful woman, that He is, in fact, the Messiah. Once again, He shows us that He approaches us with mercy, not with condemnation. The Samaritan woman had nothing to offer Jesus except a drink of water. She didn't lay out a banquet for him, nor could she have even if she wanted to.

She wasn't even trying to do her best when she met Jesus. Still, He came to her, and He used her for the glory of God. Things might have happened differently if the woman allowed herself to remain gripped in her fear and shame. Instead, she went back to town and told the people about Him. Because of this, many Samaritans believed.

Jesus doesn't teach us to hold onto our shame. Instead, He redeems us from it. Friend, His mercy is not just for other people, it's for you, too. So when you find yourself faced with those bullies, guilt and shame, ask yourself: what would Jesus tell me to do?

Are you afraid that your best isn't perfect or even good enough? Are your past mistakes holding you back? The truth is that without Christ, our efforts will never be enough, but with Him, we have no need to worry. He is ALWAYS enough, and He calls you, equips you, and walks with you as you do the work. Let go of the drive for perfection – there is no winning in that game, and instead focus on serving others with love. You cannot fall short in the Lord's eyes, so do not be afraid. He only sees His beloved daughter.

PERSPECTIVE SHIFT:

The demands and challenges we face as caregivers are ongoing, but we can reframe our experience by shifting our perspective. By learning to view our situation through the lens of God's Word and by leaning into the Truth it provides, we can begin to move from feeling fearful to hopeful, from embattled to empowered in Christ, and from unseen to unconditionally loved.

SACRIFICE: When was the last time you felt like you failed at caregiving? What happened?

HOPE: What is one thing you have learned after making a caregiving mistake?

INTERVENTION: Recognize that it is impossible to please all people all the time.

FOLLOW-UP: Relying on the biblical Truth – that Jesus is enough for us – have you been able to shift your outlook about your perceived performance?

TRUST: *Jesus, we trust that You alone are enough. We don't have to earn Your love. We don't have to prove our worthiness. You have washed our sins away with Your blood. Help us to remain in Your Truth and in Your presence.*

Amen.

PART 7

EMBRACE YOUR NEED FOR ENCOURAGEMENT

"Therefore encourage one another and build each other up, just as in fact you are doing."
– 1 Thessalonians 5:11

CHAPTER 13

UNQUALIFIED YET CALLED

"If we knew what we were doing, it would not be called research, would it?"
– Albert Einstein[1]

I had no business sitting behind that table. I was feeling both nervous and annoyed at what was shaping up to be a long day. I looked around at the mostly empty lobby and wondered how long it would take before people started trickling in, turning the silence into a low hum of conversation. This was my first day working for this company as a temporary worker – someone who is sometimes called in to cover absences or short-term assignments. You will not believe what these people wanted me to do – they sent me to the lobby and put me behind the information desk. But here's the best part: I had absolutely no information. I didn't have a building map, a directory, any knowledge of the surrounding area – nothing.

I spent the day as you might expect... apologizing and telling people, "I don't have that information." I disappointed people all day long, and by the time I left for the day, I was absolutely spent. My feelings of overwhelm, discouragement, and incompetence reared their ugly heads as soon as I realized my predicament that morning, and while I felt completely unqualified for the task, I didn't have the slightest idea what to do about it.

LIE #13: I'M UNQUALIFIED

"They say that God won't give you more than you can handle – sometimes I wish He wasn't so confident in me," my friend confided over a cup of coffee. I wanted to jump up and yell, "YES! Preach it, sister!" I've had times when I've murmured to God, "What are You thinking? I can't do this!" I've walked into situations where I was wildly unqualified for the task in front of me – at first.

Have you run up against this situation in your caregiving journey? It's not unusual to be confronted with new tasks or new ways of needing to do things that were once routine. While we may balk at something we don't feel equipped to do, we need to remember that we are smart, capable women and that we can step into any calling God gives us by relying on Him.

There are different ways we can be equipped for something. There are lots of things I am not competent to do — for instance, I'm not a brain surgeon, or a mechanic, or an Information Technology specialist. My kids know that I'm the adult in the house to go to if they are bleeding, but if they have a computer problem, I am not their girl. I AM unqualified for lots of things, but that's not usually what we are thinking about when we buy into the lie that says, "I'm not qualified." What we often believe is the misconception that we are incapable of stepping into a hard situation. Have you found yourself struggling with the intimidating feeling that God is asking too much of you? Have you perhaps been plugging along, feeling like you hit your stride, and then – God taps you on the shoulder and hands you something new?

We are often confronted with circumstances that seem daunting, and sometimes our first reaction is to shake our heads and say, "Um... no, thank you." We can usually come up with a multitude of reasons for passing on the job: I don't have time; I don't have experience; I don't have the temperament for that; I can't afford it; and – my personal favorite – someone else would be better for it. The "someone else" excuse – God has some experience with this one.

The book of Exodus tells of Moses leading his people out of slavery in Egypt. Despite God speaking directly to him, Moses still balks and makes excuses when the Lord gives him instructions:

> *"The Lord said, 'I have indeed seen the misery of my people in Egypt. I have heard them crying out because of their slave drivers, and I am concerned about their suffering. So I have come down to rescue them from the hand of the Egyptians and to bring them up out of that land into a good a spacious land, a land flowing with milk and honey – the home of the Canaanites, Hittietes, Amorites, Perizzites, Hivetes and Jebusites. And now the cry of the Israelites has reached me, and I have seen the way the Egyptians are oppressing them. So now, go. I am sending you to Pharaoh to bring my people the Israelites out of Egypt.'*
>
> *But Moses said to God, 'Who am I that I should go to Pharaoh and bring the Israelites out of Egypt?'"*
>
> *– Exodus 3:7-11*

After receiving further instructions and reassurance from God, Moses again hesitates in his obedience:

> *"Moses answered, 'What if they do not believe me or listen to me and say, 'The Lord did not appear to you'?'"*
>
> *– Exodus 4:1*

God has Moses perform tasks that the Lord uses as a demonstration of power. After Moses threw his staff onto the ground, it turned into a snake. God told Moses to reach out and pick it up by the tail. When Moses obeyed, the snake turned back to a staff in his hand. Following this, God has Moses reach into his cloak, and when he withdraws his hand, it is leprous. God then tells Moses to put his hand back into his cloak, and this time, when he withdraws his hand, it was restored. God goes on to tell Moses how to perform another sign if he faces resistance from the Egyptians, but still, Moses tries to wiggle out of his assignment:

> "Moses said to the Lord, 'Pardon your servant, Lord. I have never been eloquent, neither in the past nor since you have spoken to your servant. I am slow of speech and tongue.' The Lord said to him, 'Who gave human beings their mouths? Who makes them deaf or mute? Who gives them sight or makes them blind? Is it not I, the Lord? Now go; I will help you speak and will teach you what to say.' But Moses said, 'Pardon your servant, Lord. Please send someone else.'"
>
> – Exodus 4:10-13

Sometimes, I think we have an immediate reaction of "I'm not qualified" when we don't want to step up to the plate. I've volunteered for many things over the years, but I have also thought, *"Please pick someone else."* PTA committee chair, anyone? Perhaps, like me, you've avoided eye contact and tried to blend into the wall because you don't want to even think about adding one more commitment to your already full schedule, or maybe you're afraid that by stepping into new responsibility you make yourself vulnerable to failing in the public eye. As I've looked back at some of my experiences, I've started to wonder: is it possible that the enemy uses our insecurities against us to slow down the work with which we are tasked? Are we listening to the wrong voices – the ones that say, "You can't do this; you aren't strong enough; you aren't smart enough; you aren't patient enough"?

Hesitation is part of the human experience. Sometimes, it serves us well. For instance, we should be cautious before crossing a busy street. However, other times it encourages us to stay in our comfort zone as the enemy tries to disengage us from God's voice. Make no mistake: God's purposes will be fulfilled. While our disobedience will not affect the outcome, it may change the way in which it comes about.

The book of Esther gives us a powerful lesson on the importance of stepping into the Lord's will rather than shying away from it. King Xerxes of the Persian Empire desired a new queen, and through an unlikely set of circumstances, he selected Esther for the role, not knowing her real background as a Jew. One of the king's men had targeted Esther's uncle, Mordecai, out of anger over a perceived act of disrespect. Mordecai refused to follow the king's order that the man should be honored and bowed down to. A plot was hatched to destroy not only Mordecai but all the Jews in the kingdom. Mordecai sent word to Esther through her servant, Hathak, asking her to approach the king on behalf of the Jewish people. Let's look at what happened next:

"Hathak went back and reported to Esther what Mordecai had said. Then she instructed him to say to Mordecai, 'All the king's officials and the people of the royal provinces know that for any man or woman who approaches the king in the inner court without being summoned the king has but one law: that they be put to death unless the king extends the gold scepter to them, and spares their lives. But thirty days have passed since I was called to go to the king.'

When Esther's words were reported to Mordecai, he sent back this answer: 'Do not think that because you are in the king's house you alone of all the Jews will escape. For if you remain silent at this time, relief and deliverance for the Jews will arise from another place, but you and your father's family will perish. And who knows but that you have come to your royal position for a time such as this?'"

— Esther 4:9-14

Friend, despite how difficult your circumstances may be, I invite you to open your heart to the possibility that the Lord has called you into this caregiving journey. Perhaps you are meant for a time such as this. We can rightly recognize when we don't know what we are doing or when we feel like the task in front of us is too much to handle. What we need to remember, though, is that Jesus is enough. He is qualified. He will bring redemption, and He will empower you to do the work He calls you to do. The apostle Paul explains it here:

"Such confidence we have through Christ before God. Not that we are competent in ourselves to claim anything for ourselves, but our competence comes from God. He has made us competent as ministers of a new covenant — not of the letter but of the Spirit; for the letter kills, but the Spirit gives life."

— 2 Corinthians 3:4-6

Our qualifications do not originate with ourselves but with God. We do not walk alone. Jesus walks with us and is our advocate and encourager, our protector, and our guide. We can walk forward caring for others and loving God wholeheartedly while resting safely in the Truth of His Word. You may feel unqualified, my friend, but you are indeed called. The Lord may have been preparing you for this season in advance, or He may be equipping you as each need arises. But know this — when God calls you, He will make a way forward. Relying on Jesus, who is ultimately and completely qualified, you can lean into your calling as the Holy Spirit works in you, with you, and through you. The truth is that on our own, we are all unqualified, but with Christ, all things are possible.

PERSPECTIVE SHIFT:

The demands and challenges we face as caregivers are ongoing, but we can reframe our experience by shifting our perspective. By learning to view our situation through the lens of God's Word and by leaning into the Truth it provides, we can begin to move from feeling fearful to hopeful, from embattled to empowered in Christ, and from unseen to unconditionally loved.

SACRIFICE: How have you felt unqualified as a caregiver?

HOPE: In what way has God equipped you to step into a caregiving role, and what do you feel like you still need to learn?

INTERVENTION: Consider learning a new skill such as CPR or something else that will help you to feel confident as you give care.

FOLLOW-UP: How has educating yourself made you feel about your ability as a caregiver?

TRUST: *Heavenly Father, we know that You are our source of strength and courage. Help us to trust that You will equip us for the works to which You call us. Jesus is qualified indeed and has commissioned us to go forth in His love, sharing our compassion with His children.*

Amen.

CHAPTER 14

DOUBTING HEARTS, LOVING GOD

---

*"Doubt is a question mark; faith is an exclamation point.
The most compelling, believable, realistic stories have
included them both."*
– Criss Jami[1]

---

ears streamed down my young daughter's face as she stared at me in disbelief. After fielding several rounds of her probing, doubt-filled questions, I caved and admitted that I was, in fact, Santa Claus. She was that age: that time when all the kids at school were talking about how Santa isn't real and daring each other to ask their parents about it. My daughter, once solid in her belief of the jolly fat guy, had started to question the feasibility of such a setup.

She sat in stunned silence for a few moments as she processed the upsetting news, and then it dawned on her that Santa might not be the only character that mom had fibbed about. Once the first domino fell, the others quickly tumbled. A fresh round of tears erupted as she turned her puppy dog eyes at me and asked, "What about the Tooth Fairy?" "Yes," I replied guiltily. I could tell from the look in her eyes that she was wondering if she could trust me anymore. We took some time to talk about imagination and reality, and then we sat in uncomfortable silence. The minutes ticked by, and just when I thought I had managed to calm her down she hysterically blurted out, "Wait! Wait... *(sniff sniff)*... the Easter BUNNY?"

Like children, we, too, grow in maturity and faith, asking many questions along the way. The book of Hebrews acknowledges struggling Christians and seeks to help them become firm in their knowledge of Christ Jesus.

> *"About this we have much to say, and it is hard to explain, since you have become dull of hearing. For though by this time you ought to be teachers, you need someone to teach you again the basic principles of the oracles of God. You need milk, not solid food, for everyone who lives on milk is unskilled in the world of righteousness, since he is a child. But solid food is for the mature, for those who have their powers of discernment trained by constant practice to distinguish good from evil."*
>
> **– Hebrews 5:11-14, ESV**

Notice the author uses the words "trained by constant practice." Scripture shows us here that God recognizes our propensity to ask questions and doubt as we learn to seek and know Him. Questioning is not the same thing as disbelieving, but oftentimes, we feel as though asking questions is in direct opposition to having faith. We can feel guilty when we experience moments of doubt because we believe the next lie – that good Christians never waver.

LIE #14: IF I'M A GOOD CHRISTIAN, I WON'T DOUBT

Are you a good Christian? Did you wince just now reading that question? I don't know about you, but I have fallen prey to the trap of labels, especially that loaded one: "good." For me, "good" has been the unspoken boundary drawing lines around my behavior for years. I look at myself through the eyes of the world and try to figure out if I'm succeeding or not. It can be a harsh lens through which to see yourself. Instead of starting with how God sees me, I focus on anything I might be struggling with and somehow that becomes the newest character flaw I feel ashamed of. And while I might confide in a friend that I feel like I had a bad parenting moment, or was an impatient wife, or said an unkind word in a moment of anger, in the past I've drawn the line at confessing when I experience doubt toward God.

Doubts can be frightening. When we start to question things we believed to be true, we open the possibility that we will change our mind about something. Some doubts are minor – I remember having to repeatedly check with my young children, "Are you SURE you brushed your teeth?" Other doubts can shake our very foundations – perhaps you have questioned the loyalty of a spouse and felt the pain that comes with uncertainty. Doubt can function much like pain does; it alerts us that something needs attention.

Doubt is part of the human condition and a natural part of how we learn. Fear of a suddenly new reality can trigger a fresh wave of doubtful feelings, but I have found that sometimes the most beautiful moments are experienced in moments of doubt or questioning and behind the veil of our tears: the bedside moments, the praying and singing over a loved one during her last days, the sharing in a moment of intense relief when your friend finishes her last round of chemo. I want to encourage you to understand that questioning why someone is sick, why someone is suffering, and why God is allowing it does not separate you from His love. As long as we keep seeking His face, we are trusting in His ability to lead us through the questions and to wait patiently with us while we wrestle with competing thoughts.

Cheryl's Story:

Cheryl grew up in a large family with both brothers and sisters. She was 38 years old when her father suffered a stroke. He was bedridden, and one afternoon, Cheryl found herself in an uncomfortable predicament: she was home alone with her father, and he had to go to the bathroom. She tried to see if he could wait until someone else got home to help him, but that wasn't an option. "I had never seen him undressed," she shared. Cheryl continued describing her discomfort. "He couldn't use the urinal by himself, and I had to help him. It was the worst thing I've ever experienced – having to take care of a parent like that. My hands were shaking, and I spilled everything from the urinal on the bed and on him." Cheryl thought to herself, *"I can't do this."*

Then, encouragement came from an unlikely source as Cheryl's dad recognized her distress. He talked her through it, telling her that it was going to be okay and that they were going to get through this. Her dad, who was no doubt embarrassed about having to ask his daughter for intimate personal care, offered her a way through. He saw her struggling with not only the task of helping him use the bathroom but feeling stressed because she wanted to maintain his dignity. Her dad, in the midst of his own difficulty, modeled the love of Christ. He was more concerned with Cheryl's feelings than his own.

Cheryl, emboldened by her father's encouraging words, went into the bathroom to gather supplies. While there, she begged God for strength, and God did not disappoint. She described experiencing a sense of peace and calm that settled over her, replacing her fear and doubt, and consequently, she was able to gather up what she needed and she returned to bathe and clothe her father. In a moment that felt like a crisis, Cheryl's dad threw her a lifeline with his comforting words and reassurance that they would get through the experience together.

The point is this: we can all use a bit of encouragement when we are staring down something scary or new when we doubt ourselves or even doubt God's goodness and ability to equip us for the job at hand. There are many tasks that you will have to learn to do as a caregiver – some more unnerving than others – but you will learn as you go. That which feels nearly impossible the first time you are faced with it will likely become routine after a while.

The truth is that we long to feel seen and heard and truly known, and at the heart of it, isn't that what most doubt is about? Friend, I have found myself struggling with the scariest doubts when I was the farthest away from God. Quiet questions in my heart became loud and demanding as I tried to reconcile my understanding of the absolute love of my Heavenly Father with the hard facts of the situation on the ground: *"Don't you see me, Lord? Don't you understand how much this hurts my heart?"*

We pour out our time and energy into caring for others – giving away small pieces of ourselves every day. As we succumb to exhaustion, we lose confidence in our ability to keep caregiving. We question ourselves and may even feel uncertain about the goodness of the Lord. Support from those around us can be transformative when we find ourselves in this hollowed-out emotional space. A simple word of thanks can often be the only encouragement we need to get up and face the next day with a renewed sense of purpose and spirit. Oftentimes, our work is nearly invisible. People around us don't see us spending five hours on the phone trying to untangle a mess with health insurance benefits. They lack context to understand the crushing loneliness that creeps in when your husband doesn't remember you, and you feel like you've lost your best friend. While some of our loved ones may be hyper-aware of the situation and doing everything they can to help, others who love us can be blissfully unaware of how draining and demanding our days are – and they may remain so unless we learn to speak up and ask for help. Scripture points us to the benefits of relying on one another.

"And let us consider how we may spur one another on toward love and good deeds, not giving up meeting together, as some are in the habit of doing, but encouraging one another – and all the more as you see the Day approaching."

— Hebrews 10:24-25

It can be easy to feel like we are alone, but we need to remember that we are surrounded by our brothers and sisters in Christ. God created us to be in community, and He wants us to work together in cooperation, as different parts of the body of Christ. If you are feeling alone in your caregiving walk, I urge you to reach out and ask someone for help, support, or encouragement. It can be extremely helpful to seek the services of a professional counselor either during your caregiving journey or afterward. In addition to professional help, a friend – a sister in Christ, can be a lifeline when you are struggling with doubt, when you feel far from God. She can help you remember what God says and allow you to see that asking questions doesn't mean you aren't a faithful Christian. She can encourage you to take your doubts to God. Friends can help us walk through times of doubt, but encouragement in Christ can help us walk out of our doubt and into a place of peace and rest in the Lord. When we have doubts, we can work through them by taking them to Jesus and asking Him to work on our hearts, which Scripture says is important.

"Above all else, guard your heart, for everything you do flows from it."

— Proverbs 4:23

Everything flows from our hearts. This is such a powerful message that makes perfect sense when we think about it, for the desires of our heart influence our relationships, our decision making, and eventually, our outward actions. By anchoring ourselves in God's Word, we can learn to recognize when our thoughts are not in alignment with it. Once we recognize the lies, we can counteract them with the Truth, and by doing so, we guard our hearts. We guard our hearts against the dangers of misconceptions and untruths that put themselves in between us and our close relationship with Jesus. My friend, He wants an intimate relationship with you. He desires for you to know Him and trust Him fully so that you might live in the peace that only He can give.

Doubt is not a bad word, and it is not a surprise to God that we struggle with it from time to time. To doubt is to have questions that are colored by pain. It is normal to have questions as we step into a faith journey, whether we begin in childhood or well into our old age. And while we may hit bumps in the road, Jesus won't stop calling to us, "Come to me." He calls us forward, even through seasons of doubt. Therefore, my friend, take your doubting and loving heart and give it to the One who loves you unconditionally. He will not turn away from you – not in your strong moments and certainly not in your questioning ones – and that is the truth.

PERSPECTIVE SHIFT:

The demands and challenges we face as caregivers are ongoing, but we can reframe our experience by shifting our perspective. By learning to view our situation through the lens of God's Word and by leaning into the Truth it provides, we can begin to move from feeling fearful to hopeful, from embattled to empowered in Christ, and from unseen to unconditionally loved.

SACRIFICE: Be brave: list one or two situations or circumstances that have led you to feeling doubtful about the goodness of God.

HOPE: What would make you feel better about those situations?

INTERVENTION: Take your doubts and your questions directly to the Lord and ask for reassurance.

FOLLOW-UP: Continue this conversation with God for several days. How has He guided you?

TRUST: *Lord, help us when we walk through feelings of doubt or unbelief. Remind us that nothing can snatch us from Your mighty hand. You understand that our hearts are prone to wandering. Never stop chasing after us, Lord, and help us to stop running away when we are scared, but rather draw us deeper into a trusting relationship with You.*

Amen.

PART 8

REMAIN ROOTED IN THE LORD

"I am the vine; you are the branches. If you remain in me and I in you, you will bear much fruit; apart from me you can do nothing. If you do not remain in me, you are like a branch that is thrown away and withers; such branches are picked up, thrown into the fire and burned. If you remain in me and my words remain in you, ask whatever you wish, and it will be done for you. This is to my Father's glory, that you bear much fruit, showing yourselves to be my disciples."
– John 15:5-8

CHAPTER 15

BEYOND THE HURT

"Sometimes when you're in a dark place you think you've been buried, but you've actually been planted."
– Christine Caine[1]

*I*t felt like the sky was falling. The uncertainty of my situation and the emotional pain were so extreme that it was manifesting with physical symptoms in my body. I'd had a headache and an upset stomach for days on end, and I was so jittery that my hands shook as I tried to write in my journal. I was pouring out and pouring out and not doing anything to refill my own cup – you can guess how that turned out. "What else, Lord?" I cried out. The hits kept coming, and each painful experience served to reinforce my feeling that God had turned His back on me.

I can look back and see how God was near to me during my most painful times, but I didn't always feel like it. This is one way God has taught me about His faithfulness: I can see now what I didn't see then. The air has cleared, and my tears have dried, and suddenly what seemed so obvious to me in the moment is now revealed as the farthest thing from the truth. God does not leave us alone in our pain, but rather, is there with us.

In my exhaustion and defeat, I was sure in my belief that nothing good could ever come from what I was going through.

When we feel far from God, it can be easy to hold on to the feeling that it's all for nothing, and I certainly believed the next lie.

LIE #15: MY PAIN HAS NO PURPOSE

Jesus knows pain. Our perfect, sinless Savior has an intimate understanding of our pain, as He Himself has experienced it. Jesus was falsely accused, betrayed, handed over, arrested, denied, and disowned. Luke points us to what happened after Judas betrayed Jesus:

> *"Then seizing him, they led him away and took him into the house of the high priest. Peter followed at a distance. And when some there had kindled a fire in the middle of the courtyard and had sat down together, Peter sat down with them. A servant girl saw him seated there in the firelight. She looked closely at him and said, 'This man was with him.' But he denied it. 'Woman, I don't know him,' he said."*
>
> *— Luke 22:54-57*

In a moment of fear, Peter did what many of us do – he tried to avoid pain. He saved himself some temporary trouble, but at what cost? Peter denied even knowing Jesus, who would have felt the sting of rejection. Jesus understands our suffering because He suffered. He shares our humanity – having been sent to us as both fully man and fully God. Jesus was stripped, mocked, spit on, flogged, and beaten with fists. Jesus endured immense pain, and yet He walked through it in obedience, even to His death on the cross.

> *"Then the soldiers of the governor took Jesus into the governor's headquarters, and they gathered the whole battalion before him. And they stripped him and put a scarlet robe on him, and twisting together a crown of thorns, they put it on his head and put a reed in his*

right hand. And kneeling before him, they mocked him,
saying, 'Hail, king of the Jews!' And they spit on him
and took the reed and struck him on the head. And
when they had mocked him, they stripped him of the
robe and put his own clothes on him and led him away
to crucify him."

– Matthew 27:27-31

When the pain piles on, it can be hard for us to see the bigger picture beyond the hurt. We struggle to get through the hours, barely managing to put one foot in front of the other. Have you been there? Have you been in that place where the hits just keep coming, one bad thing after another, and you can't understand anything but the pain? The pain – that you understand — it is sharp, all-encompassing, and exhausting. Sometimes, we can't help but wonder: what's the point? What could possibly be the purpose in this anguish?

"When they came to the place called the Skull, they
crucified him there, along with the criminals – one on
his right, the other on his left. Jesus said, 'Father, forgive
them, for they do not know what they are doing.' And
they divided up his clothes by casting lots."

– Luke 23:33-34

Jesus knows what it is like to feel alone, unappreciated, and even despised. We see His suffering as the Scripture describes His time on the cross.

"From noon until three in the afternoon darkness came
over the land. About three in the afternoon Jesus cried
out in a loud voice, 'Eli, Eli, lema sabachthani?' (which
means 'My God, my God, why have you forsaken me?')."

– Matthew 27:45-46

I cannot even imagine the pain of crucifixion, as it was indeed designed to inflict a lengthy tortuous death. And yet we see that even as Jesus submitted Himself to His Father's will, He cried out – "Why have you forsaken me?" The good news is this: Jesus' crucifixion served a purpose – that's right, my friend, think about the purpose of Jesus' pain. It's EVERYTHING.

> *"For God so loved the world that he gave his one and only Son, that whoever believes in him should not perish, but have eternal life."*
>
> – John 3:16

God used Jesus' pain for His purposes, and He will use your pain too. It's difficult, if not impossible, to connect to this truth on a heart level when we are in the trenches, overwhelmed and suffering. Our situation can feel like a landscape in the aftermath of a forest fire. We take stock, looking around at scorched earth, and often have no idea how to begin again, how to move forward in our new reality. Maybe your fire is a diagnosis, a heart attack, or a serious accident that will forever change your world – whatever caused the fire, the pain sears our hearts, and we struggle to see past our immediate situation.

Do you know the benefits of a forest fire? It leads to new and abundant life as, over time, the remains of the burned brush turn into fertile soil.[2] Fresh plant life springs up and feeds growing populations of wildlife. Much like it takes years for the environment to recover from a fire, we may not see our pain at work immediately. The fact is that we may not ever understand the purpose in our pain, but that doesn't mean it is nonexistent. It just means that we don't have a full view into the workings of God.

My Aunt Eileen's Story:

My great-aunt, Eileen, had a son who was born with microcephaly – a condition in which the brain doesn't develop properly, failing to grow to a normal size. Stephen required constant care. Years later, after being reassured by the 1950s doctors that she was unlikely to have another child with the condition, Eileen gave birth to her second son, Dewey. He, too, had microcephaly. The diagnosis was devastating. Dewey lived well into his 30s – an infant in the body of a fully grown man.

I will never forget the time that Aunt Eileen and Dewey spent visiting my grandmother when I was young. It was shocking to me that someone lived like Dewey. He was blind, unable to walk, he had to be fed and diapered, and yet he was in an adult body. To be honest, I wasn't sure what to make of him at first, but my fear and alarm were quickly replaced by curiosity and then compassion as I spent time with him.

Over the years, I've heard discussions about how sad it was that Eileen was burdened with two children who needed constant care and would never really grow up. "There's no point in this suffering," my grandmother used to complain. I completely understand why she felt that way, but I had to let her in on a little secret. The few days that I spent around Dewey changed me as a person: I was suddenly aware that not everyone is healthy and able-bodied, and compassion rooted itself in my heart. I was not a significant part of Dewey's life; they visited for a few days and returned to their home in another state. But here's the thing: Dewey did play a significant role in my life, and I'm sure neither he nor my aunt ever knew the impact he had on me. Spending time around him awakened something in me that has never gone away – a desire to bring comfort and mercy to those who need it.

The short time I spent with Dewey was unremarkable to those around me, but it is one of my core memories. Sometimes, our pain and our recovery from it is used to point others around us to the Holy Lord, and we may never even know about it. Friend, I have seen miracles, I've seen small little God winks, and lots of things in between. Likewise, I've also shared in devastating loss and crippling pain that stopped me in my tracks. In retrospect I've wondered – what do we understand of laughter without the experience of tears? The truth is that no pain is too big for God to redeem, and no tears are unseen by our Heavenly Father.

The book of Ecclesiastes gives us these beautiful words:

"There is a time for everything,
And a season for every activity under the heavens:
A time to be born and a time to die,
A time to plant and a time to uproot,
A time to kill and a time to heal,
A time to tear down and a time to build,
A time to weep and a time to laugh,
A time to mourn and a time to dance,
A time to scatter stones and a time to gather them,
A time to embrace and a time to refrain from embracing,
A time to search and a time to give up,
A time to keep and a time to throw away,
A time to tear and a time to mend,
A time to be silent and a time to speak,
A time to love and a time to hate,
A time for war and a time for peace."

– Ecclesiastes 3:1-8

God is Creator of all things, and in the above passage, we are told there is a "time for everything, and a season for every activity under the heavens." God does not create by accident, and this verse explains to us that God has purpose in all things. Hope and lament can exist together. God recognizes that we will have hard times in this world, and it's okay for us to experience those emotions of sadness or mourning, but our hope remains in Jesus. We will walk through difficulty, but we can keep our eyes heavenward as we do so.

"I have seen the burden God has laid on the human race. He has made everything beautiful in its time. He

has also set eternity in the human heart; yet no one can
fathom what God has done from beginning to end."

— Ecclesiastes 3:10-11

We are safely in the hands of God and He does not waste our pain. Let's take another look at the book of Ruth:

"So Boaz took Ruth and she became his wife. When
he made love to her, the Lord enabled her to conceive,
and she gave birth to a son. The women said to Naomi,
'Praise be to the Lord, who this day has not left you
without a guardian-redeemer. May he become famous
throughout Israel! He will renew your life and sustain
you in your old age. For your daughter-in-law, who
loves you and who is better to you than seven sons, has
given him birth.'"

— Ruth 4:13-15

Ruth and Naomi seemingly get a happy ending in this story. These two women, who have walked through so much pain, are taken care of in the end, but there's more than meets the eye. The book of Ruth closes with this nod to the future:

"Then Naomi took the child in her arms and cared for
him. The women living there said, 'Naomi has a son!'
And they named him Obed. He was the father of Jesse,
the father of David."

–Ruth 4:16-17

In this way, Ruth, whose journey began with one brave decision, came together with Boaz and became part of the lineage of Jesus. The beginning of the Gospel of Matthew summarizes the ancestry this way:

"Thus there were fourteen generations in all from
Abraham to David, fourteen from David to the exile to
Babylon, and fourteen from the exile to the Messiah."

–Matthew 1:17

We see that the Lord put Ruth on a path that wove her into the family line of Jesus. Ruth – a seemingly unlikely person to show up in the ancestry of our Savior – was placed there deliberately by God. We can see the beauty in her story now, but while she was intimately familiar with her pain, she likely never imagined the beauty that would one day be born from it.

Friend, I want to encourage you to hold tightly to Jesus when you cannot see beyond your pain. The hurt you are feeling in this moment may be so intense and all-consuming that you fear you will never again find happiness and joy. For this reason, it is vitally important to remain rooted in the Lord. How do we hold fast to Jesus? We start with prayer – honest, earnest conversation with our Heavenly Father. Return to His Word, which is full of wisdom, encouragement, and joyful hope. Lean on those around you for support. As the book of Ecclesiastes reminds us: there is a season for everything under the heavens – and we can find comfort in the knowledge that God doesn't waste the season of our pain, nor will it last forever. We may or may not see His purposes for it during our earthly life, but by trusting in His goodness and relying on His promises, we can bravely move forward beyond the hurt. The truth is that God loves you dearly, and He will not waste your pain, but rather, will use it for the glory of His name.

PERSPECTIVE SHIFT:

The demands and challenges we face as caregivers are ongoing, but we can reframe our experience by shifting our perspective. By learning to view our situation through the lens of God's Word and by leaning into the Truth it provides, we can begin to move from feeling fearful to hopeful, from embattled to empowered in Christ, and from unseen to unconditionally loved.

SACRIFICE: What is the pain you are holding onto in the secret places of your heart? Take it to God (silently or aloud), and let Him hold it with you.

HOPE: What is something painful in your life that, in hindsight, you can see that God used for your good or for His glory? How does that make you feel about your current situation?

INTERVENTION: Cry out to the Lord. Be honest and vulnerable, and allow yourself to acknowledge the pain you are feeling.

FOLLOW-UP: How do you feel after being honest with God about your pain?

TRUST: *Heavenly Father, help us to understand how to navigate this broken world. We long to know why bad things happen, why people get hurt or sick, and why there is so much sadness in life. Stay by our sides as we cry, mourn, and seek answers. We love You, and we trust that You will use our pain for Your glory.*

Amen.

CHAPTER 16

LOVE LEADS ON

"That which was hard to endure is sweet to remember."
– Seneca[1]

aregiving is difficult and complicated at times, but as we've discovered together, it is also holy, honorable, and a privilege. My friend, you are doing the work – you are showing up day in and day out, acting as the hands and feet of Jesus. I want to recognize that the hours you spend providing care are precious. Your care makes a difference to your loved one, your community, and most importantly, your God. We've learned that caregiving often requires sacrifice and self-denial but that it can also strengthen you when you lean into the Truth of the Lord. Even now, as you walk this road, He is equipping you so that you may step forward, not in fear, but in confidence and with a servant's heart.

"So do not fear, for I am with you; do not be dismayed, for I am your God. I will strengthen you and help you; I will uphold you with my righteous right hand."
– Isaiah 41:10

He will strengthen us and help us, and we in turn should entrust ourselves into His loving care. It is hard to come to a place of surrender when we are trying with all our strength to maintain a semblance of control in a chaotic situation. And while it can feel scary to lay it all down at the foot of the cross, to open our hands and give our burdens over to the Lord, it is the safest thing we can do for ourselves. As we've discussed, God loves you unconditionally and infinitely and there is nothing you can do to earn it, deserve it, keep it, or lose it. His love is unshakable even when we feel the very ground quaking beneath our feet.

> "'Though the mountains be shaken, and the hills be removed, yet my unfailing love for you will not be shaken nor my covenant of peace be removed,' says the Lord, who has compassion on you."
> — Isaiah 54:10

Remember, you are a precious child of God, a daughter of the King, fearfully and wonderfully made. We need to stand on that Truth when we are feeling unseen, worthless, or dismissed. All the things in front of you that seem insurmountable are no surprise to your Heavenly Father, who goes before you in every way.

> "See what great love the Father has lavished on us, that we should be called children of God! And that is what we are! The reason the world does not know us is that it did not know him."
> — 1 John 3:1

As we've discussed throughout the pages of this book, as caregivers, we are faced with what can feel like an endless stream of decisions, which is why it's so important that we don't buy into the lie that we should know what everyone needs. When we take our decision-making skills and buttress them with scriptural truth, we can walk down a path of wise discernment. We will be faced with situations that require us to prioritize needs, both ours and the needs of others. Remember, friend, that even Jesus sought solitude and time to pray by Himself. He is our ultimate example of someone loving others and giving of Himself but also taking time to tend to His own needs.

> *"Very early in the morning, while it was still dark, Jesus got up, left the house and went off to a solitary place, where he prayed."*
>
> — Mark 1:35

Self-care is vital so that we can continue forward in our caregiving journeys, giving of ourselves without losing ourselves. God created us as special and unique women by His design, and we need to honor that by taking care of ourselves.

Together, we've learned that we don't need to stay stuck in our feelings of ineptitude or insignificance when we understand that God provides a way forward. Relying on His Word, we can be grounded in the fact that we are loved, we are known, and we do not have to walk this road alone. As challenging as caregiving can be, it is also beautiful and sacred and an honor. You are changing the life of the person you care for. It is a blessing to be entrusted with the care of one of God's precious children, and one day, you will hold these moments as special memories in your heart.

We have dispelled and deconstructed common lies and misconceptions that caregivers sometimes believe, and we have countered them with Truth. It can be hard to remember who God says we are when we feel like we are losing ourselves as we pour out our care for others. We can easily become overwhelmed when we feel like we must do everything by ourselves. It's possible we can make the one-woman show work for a while, but it is not sustainable for the long term. The Bible teaches us that we are to rely on God rather than on ourselves alone.

> *"This is what the Lord says:*
> *'Cursed is the one who trusts in man, who draws strength from mere flesh and whose heart turns away from the Lord. That person will be like a bush in the wastelands; they will not see prosperity when it comes.*

They will dwell in the parched places of the desert, in a salt land where no one lives.

But blessed is the one who trusts in the Lord, whose confidence is in him. They will be like a tree planted by the water that sends out its roots by the stream. It does not fear when heat comes; its leaves are always green. It has no worries in a year of drought and never fails to bear fruit.'"

— Jeremiah 17:5-8

God will meet us in our desert places of despair and exhaustion and lead us to a place of peace and renewal. When we feel like we can't keep going, He will nurture us with His Holy Spirit. He will lead us to life-giving water, and He will be our strength.

"I can do all this through him who gives me strength."

— Philippians 4:13

Jesus gives us strength. When you run headfirst into the reality that we are faced with exceedingly hard things in this life, remember that you are not expected to power through by your own determination and willpower. In this broken world, we are faced with sickness and infirmity and even death, and it's easy to feel angry when we feel like the good things in our lives have been taken from us. None of us walk through life completely unscathed by the hurts of this world – and Jesus didn't escape them, either. But as we've discussed, this is good news! Jesus understands and has compassion for you. He will meet you in your moments of anger or frustration or despair – you need only to turn to Him.

"Look to the Lord and his strength; seek his face always."

–1 Chronicles 16:11

Seek Him first and follow His lead by showing mercy to others. It's easy to get discouraged or even disheartened when other people don't show any sign of gratitude or appreciation for our hard work. In fact, it can be downright maddening, but we need to keep in mind that our value and our contribution is not dependent on the opinions of other people. Scripture points out that God knows our hearts better than we do.

> *"If our hearts condemn us, we know that God is greater than our hearts, and he knows everything."*
>
> –1 John 3:20

Walk out of the shadow of condemnation and find freedom in Christ. When you feel unqualified, doubtful, or lost in the pain – the Truth of God is your escape route. These common lies we believe are strong, but God is all-powerful, and nothing is beyond His mighty reach. These lies serve to support one another, for if we believe even one, it leads to the next. Remember, when we fail to start with understanding who God is and who He says we are, we are at risk of drifting from other truths, and we find ourselves weighed down and held back.

By breaking free from even one of these lies, we awaken our hearts to all the possibilities that God puts before us. You are doing holy work that is precious in the sight of the Lord, my friend, and you deserve to find freedom and rest in Christ, who loves you dearly. What you do is making a difference every single day.

You are seen, my friend, even when you feel invisible. Caregiving often happens behind the curtain, out of sight, but God sees you. With every small act of kindness and care, you are changing the world for your loved one, and I, for one, am grateful for you. I encourage you to continue on...through the fatigue and exasperation that can come with caregiving and be encouraged... for you are an essential worker in God's kingdom.

> *"Whatever you do, work at it with all your heart, as working for the Lord, not for human masters, since you know that you will receive an inheritance from the Lord as a reward. It is the Lord Christ you are serving."*
>
> –Colossians 3:23-24

As we conclude our journey together through this book, I want to remind you that you are now going forth with the power and presence of the Holy Spirit who is with you always. None of us know exactly what our journey will look like, but we do know this: Jesus walks with us. As you step forward, He will continue to match your every step. You can move ahead in His strength; He holds you when you're weak and weary, reminding you of who you are in Him. Thank you for spending this precious time with me and entrusting me as your guide. I want to send you off with one final perspective shift, the only one that really matters: God's Word and a prayer.

> *"Therefore, since we are surrounded by such a great cloud of witnesses, let us throw off everything that hinders and the sin that so easily entangles. And let us run with perseverance the race marked out for us, fixing our eyes on Jesus, the pioneer and perfecter of faith. For the joy set before him he endured the cross, scorning its shame, and sat down at the right hand of the throne of God. Consider him who endured such opposition from sinners, so that you will not grow weary and lose heart."*
> **– Hebrews 12:1-3**

Heavenly Father, You are so good and gracious to us. Our hearts cry out for Your presence, and we pray that You will rain Your mercy down upon us as we walk through our caregiving journeys. Turn our eyes away from the untruths of this world and rather show us Your Truth, Lord. Let us stand firm on the saving grace of Christ, who died that we might live. We are so grateful. We trust You and pray that You might use us to shine Your light to those around us so that Your love might be felt by all. Remain with us as we endure all You set before us, moving ever onward with love and in service of Christ Jesus, in whose name we pray.

Amen.

RESOURCES

CAREGIVER SUPPORT:
Family Caregiver Alliance
https://www.caregiver.org/
Administration for Community Living
https://acl.gov/
U.S. Department of Health and Human Services
https://www.hhs.gov/programs/providers-and-facilities/
resources-for-caregivers/index.html
Rosalynn Carter Institute for Caregivers
https://rosalynncarter.org/
Caregiver Action Network
https://www.caregiveraction.org/

SPECIALTY CAREGIVER SUPPORT:

Alzheimer's Disease and Dementia:
Alzheimer's Association of America
https://www.alz.org/
Alzheimer's Foundation of America
https://alzfdn.org/

Brain Injury:
Brain Injury Association of America
https://www.biausa.org/brain-injury/community/caregiver-
information-center

Cancer:

American Cancer Society
https://www.cancer.org/cancer/caregivers.html

Heart Disease:

American Heart Association
https://www.heart.org/en/health-topics/heart-failure/
living-with-heart-failure-and-managing-advanced-hf/
help-for-heart-failure-caregivers

Stroke:

American Stroke Association
https://www.stroke.org/-/media/Stroke-Files/
Caregiver-Support/Caregivers-Guide-to-Stroke/
CaregiverGuideToStroke_2020.pdf

DOMESTIC ABUSE:

National Coalition Against Domestic Violence
HTTPS://NCADV.ORG/RESOURCES
National Domestic Violence Hotline
HTTPS://WWW.THEHOTLINE.ORG

FIND A COUNSELOR:

American Psychological Association
https://locator.apa.org/
American Association of Christian Counselors
https://aacc.net/

HOSPICE CARE:

Hospice Foundation of America
https://hospicefoundation.org/End-of-Life-Support-and-
Resources/Coping-with-Terminal-Illness/How-to-Choose

Notes Page

Chapter 1: Value Beyond Earning

1. Rosalynn Carter. *"There are four kinds of people in the world…"* Retrieved from https://rosalynncarter.org.

Chapter 2: Caregivers are Kingdom Workers

1. Wilde, Oscar. *The Picture of Dorian Gray*. Ward, Lock & Co., 1891.
2. AARP. *Caregiving in the United States*. Retrieved from https://www.aarp.org/content/dam/aarp/ppi/2020/05/full-report-caregiving-in-the-united-states.doi.10.26419-2Fppi.00103.001.pdf.
3. U.S. Census Bureau. *Population Projections 2018*. Retrieved from https://www.census.gov/newsroom/press-releases/2018/cb18-41-population-projections.html.
4. AARP. *Valuing the Invaluable*. Retrieved from https://www.aarp.org/content/dam/aarp/ppi/2023/3/valuing-the-invaluable-2023-update.doi.10.26419-2Fppi.00082.006.pdf
5. AARP. Valuing the Invaluable. Retrieved from https://www.aarp.org/content/dam/aarp/ppi/2023/3/valuing-the-invaluable-2023-update.doi.10.26419-2Fppi.00082.006.pdf
6. AARP. *Valuing the Invaluable*. Retrieved from https://www.aarp.org/content/dam/aarp/ppi/2023/3/valuing-the-invaluable-2023-update.doi.10.26419-2Fppi.00082.006.pdf

7. AARP. *Caregiving in the United States.* Retrieved from https://www.aarp.org/content/dam/aarp/ppi/2020/05/full-report-caregiving-in-the-united-states.doi.10.26419-2Fppi.00103.001.pdf

8. AARP. *Caregiving in the United States.* Retrieved from https://www.aarp.org/content/dam/aarp/ppi/2020/05/full-report-caregiving-in-the-united-states.doi.10.26419-2Fppi.00103.001.pdf

Chapter 3: The Comparison Trap

1. Theodore Roosevelt. *"Comparison is the thief of joy."* Retrieved from https://www.azquotes.com/quote/501479#google_vignette. While a primary source is not available, the quote is widely attributed to Theordore Roosevelt.

Chapter 4: Holding On and Letting Go

1. Corrie Ten Boom. *"Never be afraid to trust an unknown future to a known God."* Retrieved from https://www.brainyquote.com/quotes/corrie_ten_boom_381184.

2. Strong, James. *The New Strong's Expanded Exhaustive Concordance of the Bible.* Thomas Nelson Publishers, 2010.

Chapter 5: Beyond the Superwoman Syndrome

1. Lynda Carter. *"There is a part of Wonder Woman inside me..."* Retrieved from https://www.brainyquote.com/quotes/lynda_carter_912014.

2. Christianity.com. *The Importance and Meaning of a Kinsman-Redeemer.* Retrieved from https://www.christianity.com/wiki/bible/importance-and-meaning-of-a-kinsman-redeemer.html.

3. Enduringword.com. *Ruth Makes An Appeal.* Retrieved from https://enduringword.com/bible-commentary/ruth-3/

4. CDC. *Health Effects of Social Isolation and Loneliness.* Retrieved from https://www.cdc.gov/social-connectedness/

risk-factors/?CDC_AAref_Val=https://www.cdc.gov/
emotional-wellbeing/social-connectedness/loneliness.
htm

Chapter 6: Self-care in Seasons of Sacrifice

1. Roosevelt, Eleanor. *You Learn by Living: Eleven Keys for a More Fulfilling Life.* Harper & Brothers, 1960.
2. Delta Aviation. *In Flight Safety Video.* Retrieved from https://trajectoryaviationnetworktv.wordpress.com/2017/06/01/blog-post-title/
3. AARP. *Valuing the Invaluable.* Retrieved from https://www.aarp.org/content/dam/aarp/ppi/2023/3/valuing-the-invaluable-2023-update.doi.10.26419-2Fppi.00082.006.pdf

Chapter 7: Adapting Through the Overwhelm

1. Napoleon Bonaparte. *"If you want a thing done well, do it yourself."* Retrieved from https://www.brainyquote.com/quotes/napoleon_bonaparte_108864.
2. Caregiver.org. *Caregiver Statistics: Demographics.* Retrieved from https://www.caregiver.org/resource/caregiver-statistics-demographics/
3. Desilu Productions. *I Love Lucy.* Created by Jess Oppenheimer, performances by Lucille Ball, Desi Arnaz, Vivian Vance, and William Frawley, CBS, 1951–1957.

Chapter 8: The Power of One More Step

1. Winston Churchill. *"If you're going through hell, keep going."* Retrieved from https://www.brainyquote.com/quotes/winston_churchill_103788.
2. FEMA. *National Preparedness Goal.* Retrieved from https://www.fema.gov/sites/default/files/2020-06/national_preparedness_goal_2nd_edition.pdf

Chapter 9: Overcoming Exasperation

1. Gerrold, David. *An Assortment of Fictitious Lives.* New English Library, 2011.
2. Thegospelcoalition.org. *Invitation to Ruth.* Retrieved from https://www.thegospelcoalition.org/commentary/ruth/

Chapter 10: Grace in Anguish

1. Powell, Colin. *It Worked for Me: In Life and Leadership.* HarperCollins, 2012.

Chapter 11: Beyond Recognition

1. Franklin, Benjamin. *Poor Richard's Almanack.* The U.S.C. Publishing Co. 1914.
2. Britannica.com. *Schadenfreude.* Retrieved from https://www.britannica.com/topic/schadenfreude

Chapter 12: Breaking Free from the Fear of Falling Short

1. Thomas A. Edison. *"I have not failed. I've just found 10,000 ways that won't work."* Retrieved from https://www.brainyquote.com/quotes/thomas_a_edison_132683 This is a summation of a 1921 interview with *Cosmopolitan* magazine.

Chapter 13: Unqualified Yet Called

1. Albert Einstein. "If we knew what we were doing, it would not be called research, would it?" Retrieved from https://www.brainyquote.com/quotes/albert_einstein_148837

Chapter 14: Doubting Hearts, Loving God

1. Jami, Criss. *Killosophy.* Killosopher Apparel, 2015.

Chapter 15: Beyond the Hurt

1. Christine Caine. *"Sometimes when you're in a dark place, you think you've been buried, but you've actually been*

planted." Retrieved from https://www.goodreads.com/quotes/7072229-sometimes-when-you-re-in-a-dark-place-you-think-you-ve.

2. Nationalgeographic.org. *The Ecological Benefits of Fire.* Retrieved from https://education.nationalgeographic.org/resource/ecological-benefits-fire/

Chapter 16: Love Leads On

1. While attributed to many authors, the phrase aligns closest with Letters to Lucillus by the Roman philosopher Seneca.

Author Bio

Amy Chastain is a Registered Nurse and caregiver advocate with over 15 years of hands-on experience. A committed follower of Jesus and ministry leader, Amy is passionate about the hard and holy work of caregiving. She has personally navigated the day-to-day challenges of this role and is dedicated to helping others understand their God-given value and manage caregiving without losing themselves. At home, Amy is a wife and mother of four, with a heart for equipping and encouraging those who care for others. Her approach blends practical guidance with spiritual support, making her a beloved mentor in the caregiving community.